66 *Paul Annacone has been blessed with talent and surrounded by it his entire life. He's learned superlative lessons from terrific coaches and competitors, and in this book he passes on to you all that he's admired and absorbed—as a student, a player, and a world class coach.* " – MARY CARILLO Peabody & Sports Emmy award-winning commentator and journalist

66 *If I could sum up my time working with Paul in three words it would be:* process not outcome. *He was brilliant at ingraining good habits on the practice court, emphasizing the need to trust your game and then executing that plan on the match court—this book goes through the steps to help you reach your potential & trust your process.* " – TIM HENMAN
Former British No. 1

More praise for *Coaching for LIFE*

66 *This book was hard to put down! Paul's philosophies, anecdotes, and wisdom are unparalleled... If you want a recipe to bring out the best in yourself, this book is for you!*" – CHRIS EVERT

International Hall of Fame Inductee 1995 | Former No. 1 in the world | 157 career titles, including Two Australian Open titles • Seven French Open titles • Three Wimbledon titles • Six U.S. Open titles

66 *What a terrific book! Paul hits on the key aspects to help anyone set up a plan to reach their potential. A fun read with great application.* " — TRACY AUSTIN

Former No. 1 in the world | Two-time U.S. Open champion

66 *You may come for the stories of Sampras, Federer and more but you'll also take away the valuable life lessons Paul shares from his wealth of tennis experience.* " — JIM COURIER

- Two-time Australian Open champion
- Two-time French Open champion
- Wimbledon and U.S. Open finalist
- Former World No. 1 (1992 and 1993)

66 *...It's great that Paul is sharing the experiences from his playing days as well as the philosophies he used while coaching some of the all-time greats. This book is a wonderful resource for anyone who wants to reach their potential, both on and off the tennis court. A must read.* "

— LINDSAY DAVENPORT

- Australian Open champion 2000
- Wimbledon champion 1999
- U.S. Open champion 1998
- Former No. 1 in the world
- International Tennis Hall of Fame Inductee 2014

66 *Any kid who takes his/her tennis seriously should read this. Same goes for parents too...something for everyone.* " — MARTINA NAVRATILOVA

- 167 WTA career singles titles
- 18 Grand Slam singles titles
- No. 1 in the world for 332 weeks

66 *Finally a book that is easy to understand from a former top tennis player and a successful coach whose incredible knowledge is now out for all to read.* " — PAT RAFTER

Former World No. 1 July 1999 | Davis Cup Champion Australian Team 1999 | U.S. Open champion, 1997, '98 Wimbledon finalist 2000, '01 | Former Australian Davis Cup captain

Coaching
for LIFE

IRIE
BOOKS

A Guide to Playing, Thinking and Being the Best You Can Be

Coaching
for LIFE

PAUL
ANNACONE

A special thanks to:
Ray Giubilo - tennisphotographer.com
Marianne Bevis - flickr.com/photos/mariannebevis/
Danny Moloshok - molophoto.com
Michael Baz - bazimages.com
Arnie Slater/Associated Newspapers - Shutterstock
Peter McCabe - petermccabephotography.com
Stephanie Myles

Images courtesy of:
Eric Feferberg/AFP/Getty Images
Clive Brunskill/Getty Images Sport/Getty Images
Michael Regan/Getty Images Sport/Getty Images
Alex Livesey/Getty Images Sport/Getty Images
Julien Finney/Getty Images Sport/Getty Images
New York Post Archives/New York Post Archives/Getty Images
Mathew Stockman/Getty Images Sport/Getty Images
Arnie Slater/Associated Newspapers/Shutterstock
Mark Baker/AP Photo/AP Images
Kathy Willens/AP Photo/AP Images
Marty Lederhandler/AP Photo/AP Images
Adobe Stock
Morguefile.com

Every effort has been made to trace the copyright holders and obtain permission to reproduce photography. Please contact the publisher with inquiries or information relating to images within.

Irie Books
Santa Fe, New Mexico
gahausman@earthlink.net

Cover and interior design:
ital art by Mariah Fox | mariahfox.com

ISBN 13: 9781633843820
First Edition
10 9 8 7 6 5 4 3 2 1

To Mom & Dad

You opened the door of opportunity in my life. Thanks to you it's been a wonderful journey and your selfless sacrifices have allowed so many of my dreams to become reality, with love.

Table of
CONTENTS

Foreword

n 1995, Paul Annacone quietly became my coach and the key-sounding partner in a team that would span seven years and nine Grand Slam titles. It was clear to me that Paul knew what I was all about. Like me, he embraces the quiet way. We really click in that way. Paul came to know me better than anyone else in the game. Paul is not a big rah-rah guy. He does not throw a lot of senseless verbiage at you—so take what he says to heart, as I did. It helped me win a lot of majors and a lot of tournaments.

Paul knows how to bring out excellence in you and your game, by keeping things simple rather than ramping up an occasion. His strategies worked time and time again. And when I was down in 2002, it was Paul's post-Wimbledon conversation with me that rallied me back to win my final title that same year. If you buy into Paul's mantra of believing in the process and trust that it will lead you to the result, then this book is a great book for you, because everyone can use these themes to excel.

Not just an observer from the side of the court, Paul also played, and is always quick to remind me that he beat me the only time we ever faced each other. Paul quietly pushed me to play a certain way; he pushed me to attack, chip and charge, and impose my will on my opponents. He wasn't looking for the limelight, he wasn't looking for the attention or the credit. But deep down in me, I know what he meant for my career. Paul has given me a lifetime of memories and lessons, all of which I will carry with me every day. He never got the credit he deserves. I hope this book will help do that. Thanks, Paul.

- PETE SAMPRAS

Introduction

T ennis players, coaches and parents believe that my life has been devoted to building champions. Actually, that is only partially true. I believe that a more meaningful part of my career has been in the development of championship people—people who went on to contribute to humanity; people who understood that it was within their power to improve the lives of others.

Paul Annacone is one of those individuals of whom I am most proud. His book is a "must-read" because it's real. It exposes the real challenges that a youngster faces as he develops into a responsible adult. But, make no mistake, this development comes with indecision, fear, failure, disappointment, and ultimately an awakening—the realization that, through all of these difficulties, you can succeed.

Paul began playing tennis as a young boy living in Long Island, New York. Each day that he practiced, he went home to a loving family and familiar surroundings. His life was very average until he made the monumental decision to move to Florida to focus on his tennis game. My good friend Mike DePalmer Sr. and I welcomed him to the Nick Bollettieri Tennis Academy. We mentored him and adopted him as one of the family. It's important to understand that this was a new idea. It was the first live-in tennis academy in the world. I was routinely criticized as a stern taskmaster who managed a prison camp for aspiring young tennis players.

Paul went on to receive a full scholarship to the University of Tennessee, again under the tutelage of Tennessee coach Mike DePalmer. He went onto the ATP Tour where, in 1985, he achieved a career-high ranking of No. 12 in the world. He retired in 1995 to begin what became a stellar coaching career. Paul has coached Pete Sampras, Roger Federer, Tim Henman, and most recently Sloane Stephens. He was coach for the Lawn Tennis Association, coach of Great Britain's Davis Cup Team, and managing director of the USTA's Player Development Program.

When you read this book you will see how focus and determination—along with a good team—can overcome the odds. Paul and his team have always had a "we can do it" attitude, and this book is not merely a tutorial on tennis—but rather—through will and sheer determination—a tutorial on life itself!

- NICK BOLLETTIERI

Notes

NOTES OF A COACH: PAUL ANNACONE

n the summer of 1995, just prior to the U.S. Open, I had a conversation with Pete Sampras in one of the many hotel rooms we occupied during our seven-and-a-half years working together. His thoughts, always clear and deep, resonate in my mind today.

There were two key topics: one was Andre Agassi's terrific run that summer where he did not lose a match leading into the U.S. Open. The other was the tragic situation of Pete's former coach, Tim Gullikson, who was battling brain cancer.

As the conversation unfolded, we touched on human nature. How when people are feeling good and everything is optimal, much can be achieved: But also about how to deal with life when there seems to be nothing but adversity.

As a 23-year-old tennis champion, Pete had never been in a situation like this—his best friend was fighting for his life and, at the same time, his red-hot tennis rival was demolishing every opponent he met on the court. Yes, to be sure, Pete was looking at "the wall of adversity." It was an extremely challenging time in his life. To some—in fact, most—

this wall might have been insurmountable.

But I remember Pete saying, "Tennis is easy when things are going well and everything is clicking. But I like to see what happens when players have to deal with adversity… I like to see what happens when the pressure is on and the chips are down. That's when you see what they are made of."

The wall of adversity, as I call it, is a metaphor for life.

In that moment, I knew I was lucky to be working with someone who was a master at excelling when things weren't perfect. Pete's perspective and clarity always impressed me, both as a friend and a coach, but I believe it was during this conversation that the seed of *Coaching for Life* was planted.

I realized writing the book might answer a question that was knocking around in my mind. "What makes the great so great, and what can we learn from their level of excellence? What can we learn from them about finding success for ourselves?"

As I started writing, I began to see a recipe that could be used by any one of us, so that we might bring the very best out of ourselves. This book then is about succeeding at whatever you most want to do in life.

It all hinges on dealing with adversity and the complications that come from it. We often say, "Don't sweat the details," but it is those very things that tend to drag us down when we hit the wall.

Coaching for Life is not about the sport of tennis as much as it is a process-oriented journey based on the sport of tennis. It is the life I have lived, and the front row seat from which I have watched some of the greatest players compete on the greatest courts in the world. But it is also something that can be applied to our own day-to-day lives.

In sharing what I have learned, and what I have observed on the court, I can help you—regardless of the challenges presented by adversity—to cut through the details, and traverse the wall.

What I've drawn together here, through recollection, anecdote, and personal encounter, is a useful "how-to" on succeeding at whatever you most want to do in your own life.

❝ *The man who has no imagination has no wings.* **❞**
  - MUHAMMAD ALI

1.

The Dream

n my life, I have been extremely lucky. I pursued my dream early on, and have followed it now for 30 years. Moreover, I have spent much of that time helping others achieve their dream. In many ways, being a coach has been the most fulfilling of all.

Throughout my time with Pete Sampras, Tim Henman, and Roger Federer, I helped shape the paradigms for success that, against all odds, made it possible for these unique athletes to rise above the pressure-packed, complex, and often negative environments that are the normal bill of fare for the modern professional athlete.

How does one survive in such a tightly wired, and in a sense, unforgiving world, which rates everything according to one thing—performance under pressure?

My recipe for success is a series of patterns or perhaps structures that can be used by anyone in daily life. We can use these basic paradigms to be more productive, more successful, and even to live happier, healthier, and more secure lives.

In each of us there is a secret reservoir of dreams fed by what we see and what we do, and also by observing others. Some of us have had such dreams and ambitions since childhood. Many of us have not acted upon them, and so they linger just out of reach in our unconscious mind. How can we find and recapture, our deepest ambitions? Moreover, how can we shape them so they can become a reality?

Sampras' majestic serve, Australian Open 2002 .

The first step—in any worthwhile endeavor—is to approach it with an understanding of who you are. The ancient adage, "Know thyself" is still the rudiment, the basic rubric, and the cornerstone of all beginnings. We should ask ourselves: *Who am I? Where am I going? Who is with me?* These are questions that are so fundamental, that when we are answering them we may quickly come to that part of the dream that is possibly eluding us… *What do I want to do?*

Answering that, we move on to the second step: devising a simple template with short- and long-term goals for success. Call it an outline, call it "notes to myself," whatever you call it, it's the bottom line… *What I want to do and how I want to go about doing it.* The way, in other words, that works best given who you are, where you're going, and who's with you in this pursuit of excellence.

The third step is the easiest to perceive and the hardest to achieve. For it is simply—to believe in yourself to such a degree that you can say as easily as Pete did during his entire career, "I want to get there."

The thing about Pete is, he was completely, almost serenely, confident that he would accomplish his dream when he said, in June of 2002, "One more major title."

"You can do it, no doubt," I said to Pete. "In fact it could be more than one more, if you put your mind to it."

For Pete, winning the U.S. Open was a realistic goal. It began, as it should have, with confidence, courage, and a clear, undivided focus. But on top of that, Pete drew upon his ability to visualize that which others cannot fully see. That which, to some, was just a hazy dream, he turned into a material reality. Did he see himself kissing the trophy? I can't say, nor could he, but as far as the steps he needed to take to get to that place of honor, he was already moving forward, as if with a full force gravitational attraction. He *would* meet that eventuality—or rather *inevitability.* And that factor is what makes all the difference in making your dream come true.

66 *Life is a succession of lessons which must be lived to be understood.* **"**
– HELEN KELLER

2.

Lesson Learned

A t the age of 14, the thought of joining my peers, who were also my competitors, at the Nick Bollettieri Tennis Academy was both exciting and daunting. Nick was a well-known coach, his prestigious academy had just been born, and he and it were there to help players reach their full potential.

To achieve this, Nick had to create an environment for the best players to move on to the professional tour. For others, the experience at the academy would earn them college scholarships.

I had no idea which category I would fall into but I left home with an internal debate going on inside my head. I lived in East Hampton, New York, a small town where I had a bunch of great friends who were more or less "normal"—which was also how I thought of myself. So here I was about to leave normal behind, about to give up the familiar world I loved, and plunge into the risky unknown.

There was a certain sense of sacrifice in this decision and I looked upon it with anxiety as I wondered (and feared) how I would be at the academy. *Would I fit in? Would they like me? How good a player would I be?*

This conflict stayed with me for many months after I'd made the decision to accept the challenge of a lifetime. The inner competitor in me was strong, I had a dream, and I knew what it was, and once I committed myself to something I dug in and did it.

I remember my first day on court. I saw many of the best young tennis players in the country all in one place, and this, for me, was the cutting edge of excitement. But in a matter of moments, my worries melted away. Racket in hand, I was in the moment, in the game. There was no more speculation. No more hesitation. I was there. And I loved being there.

But then, when night came and it was time to go back to the solitude of my room, reality set in.

I was alone.

Here I was with all these truly great competitors, all of whom were being driven by Nick, a hardline disciplinarian and old school Italian who did not accept excuses, lack of focus, or any effort less than maximum, and suddenly I felt very alone in all of this. What a challenge—the coach, the kids, the new environment. Nick was scary. I hated to admit it, and I was scared.

After about two weeks in, I was sitting in my room with tears in my eyes, thinking, *this is too much*. Where was the old, easy comfortable life of East Hampton High School? Where were all those familiar friends I used to hang out with? Moreover, where was my family with whom I always shared so much? All of it seemed so far away. I called my parents. This was my introduction to the wall of adversity—I was getting a first-hand view of a huge challenge and some of life's complex ingredients.

"Mom," I said, "I don't think I want to stay here."

"But—why?"

I fumbled for the words, the feelings. "Well, it's all tennis here, all structure, all discipline…" I paused, wondering what to say next. Then, "I just miss being at home and being with my friends."

"Paul," she replied in a firm voice. "You just got there. Keep going, things will get better. It's too early to come to any conclusions now."

I got off the phone, and strangely, I was suddenly less on the fence about the whole thing. It seemed to me, I could hang in there a bit and see how it all worked out. There was no real way of knowing but things might get more comfortable and I might become more resilient and self-sufficient.

Some weeks passed. Things were going OK.

Then, one day Nick came storming out of the Colony Beach tennis shop, screaming at us. Whenever the kids saw Nick barrel through the doorway towards the courts, the whole place changed. Nick was a master at imposing discipline, albeit through fear, but anyway, it always worked.

Suddenly there were no more sloppy shots, no more fooling around—it was all work, no play, but it was also incredible to see so many kids snap to attention and play their best.

Nick stomped over to Court Two where I was. He came over to me and got right up in my face.

"Look," he said. "You have all the talent in the world, but you're just a… Momma Luke." I'm spelling it now just the way he said it, and believe me, only a true Italian could say it that way and rub it in the way he did. I knew enough to keep my mouth shut and just listen.

"You have to get tougher," he said.

Funny he should say that because I thought my game *was tough*.

"You have to stay focused, you have to work, Paul. This is life, this is excellence, and there's no room for a Momma Luke here. There's no room!"

I was stunned. And embarrassed. Everyone looking at me. I just wanted to slip away and hide.

And I wanted to scream, *What do you know?!* But, later on, when I thought about it, I realized Nick saw something in me that I *did not*, and probably, without help, *could not*, see for myself. And it occurred to me that I was getting more mature and more disciplined, and that Nick's rants had a purpose—a sharp edge, but a purposeful one.

One day after I'd just won a tough match and was thinking that nothing could hurt me at that moment, Nick drove by, and when he saw me, slammed on the brakes.

"You better stop wasting your time, and get serious," he called out in front of everyone. His voice had a cutting edge. "You'll go nowhere unless you buckle down..."

I was shocked and angry at the same time. But at least he hadn't called me a Momma Luke. I thought: *What the hell, I just won a tough match in order to get to the semifinals of a tournament and Nick's giving me grief!*

But, again, a little later I resolved a few things. *Tomorrow I'm going to be a wall, mentally and physically—no mistakes, no let ups, no bullshit!*

The next day I beat one of my biggest rivals 6-0, 6-0. It was the first time I truly understood what real mettle was all about, and the effect of clarity of purpose. *Purpose, commitment,* and *belief* became the mantra of my tennis career.

Looking back, I can now say with deep gratitude, "Thank you, Nick."

He is, was, and always will be a genius coach, and I am forever indebted to him. So many lessons, so many roads. But when I think back, he was the first one who really took me and shook me, and woke me up. I love the guy, and that's no Momma Luke talking either. Lesson learned.

66 *Do not let what you cannot do interfere with what you can do.* **99**
– JOHN WOODEN

3.

The Power
of Belief

T he world of tennis is a world of strategy structured by concerted planning which serves as the road map for achieving goals. Having a long-term objective, as well as a series of short-term plans, is vital.

At the beginning of the tennis season, a coach and a player sit down to map out the tournament schedule.

A training program of on-court and off-court requirements is laid out along with necessary rest and recovery periods. Every tournament is different, so the paradigm here is set up according to the schedule of the tournaments. Technical, tactical, physical and mental training are all melded into the overall design of the program. These are the basic components of the long-term plan.

Very few, if any – covered the net with the skill and dexterity of Tim Henman, poetry in motion.

However, a second part of this is on-court strategy created for a specific practice or a match; this is a short-term rather than a long-term plan outlined in advance for each event. Both are important and both can be modified, if necessary. But you have to keep in mind what the primary and complete goal is, and make sure it is still in line with the dream. It has to be seamless—outline and plan, goal and dream.

HOW TO PLAN LIKE TIM HENMAN

A great example in the tennis world of someone who stuck to his plan is British tennis champion, Tim Henman.

In late October of 2003, I received a call from then-29-year-old year Tim Henman. We discussed where he was in his career, what he wanted to do, and how best to get there. Tim was ranked just outside the top 40 in the world but before that had been a perennial top 10 player throughout his career.

We had a great conversation but I did not hear a clear plan or, strangely enough, any kind of iron-clad belief in himself.

I said, "Listen, Tim, you have great talent, great energy, great optimism, and there's no

"IF YOU CAN MEET WITH TRIUMPH AND DISASTER
AND TREAT THOSE TWO IMPOSTORS JUST THE SAME

These words hang over the entrance to the biggest stage in the tennis world: Centre Court, Wimbledon.

reason you can't get back in the top 10."

There was a slight pause, and then Tim said, "What would you do if you were me?"

"I'd make a plan and then get after it," I told him.

"Sounds great," he said. "So tell me your thoughts about my game, my plan, and my process…"

We then discussed a number of strategic options, ways for Tim to do what he does best on the tennis court. I reminded him that this was a *process,* not a *quick fix.* We talked about how your plan has to be doable, and then you have to actually go do it.

But we also spoke about belief. Not only believing in oneself, but in the logical and consistent belief in right action, and right reward, that leads to total success, as opposed to partial achievement. The process must be visualized, acted upon, but most of all, have buy-in from the player. It must enter the mind and heart and bloodstream of the one who has adopted it.

It is just shy of being a kind of religion—if one defines this as devotion to an incontrovertible belief in a certain universal power, and that this power is within as well as outside oneself, then the idea of belief in something, virtually anything, is all-important to successful living, working, and being. It is much more than confidence.

We had subsequent calls, Tim and I, during which we went over his style of play. A versatile man if there ever was one, Tim was a great mover, volleyer, and total athlete.

Verbally, we sketched out simple themes that would work best for him, given his extraordinary athleticism—getting inside the court, taking the ball early, ending up at the net and taking the opponent's time away. These were all part of Tim's dreaded arsenal of well-wrought skills.

During practice, Tim used his ironic, and sometimes absurd, sense of humor to keep things lively. He would constantly hit balls slow and high up the middle so as not to "risk" a miss, or stand way behind the baseline and just run around blocking the ball back up the middle. This was, of course, the antithesis of what I wanted him to do. All for the sake of amusement, all to keep me on my toes, and make me smile, as I shook my head at his clowning. (Note: take yourself seriously. But don't take yourself *so* seriously. As a coach once said, "Everybody can practice, few can play.")

Tim implemented things every day with his constant, optimistic, upbeat, happy-go-lucky personality. Whether he was giving his physio, Johan DeBeer, a bucket of grief about running sprints, or extra core work for his ailing back, or bantering with me in his sardonic way about hitting extra serves to targets (which I inevitably became!), the work was done and done with joy, a spring in the step and a clear vision of what we were there to accomplish.

In October of 2003, only a few weeks into our discussions, Tim went out and won the Paris Masters where he beat Gustavo Kuerten, Roger Federer and Andy Roddick. It was an amazing run for Tim and, interestingly, it was only the beginning.

In 2004, Tim reached the semifinals of the French Open and the semifinals of the U.S. Open. In less than 12 months his ranking went from the top 40 to No. 4 in the world. A victorious end result and a testimony to the *power of belief.*

In evaluating Tim as a player you might recall that as an average-size man, perhaps slighter than most of the top players of his era, Tim did not have a "killer shot"—a huge serve or massive forehand. But what he did have—and this is important in seeing the whole athlete—was a great mind for tennis. Add to this his superior speed, deft movement, and agility along with one of the best volleys on tour. Joined together, his skills were the equal of a so-called killer shot.

Even though Tim reached the semifinals of the French Open, the critics underestimated him on clay courts. This might have been due to the fact that he didn't play like a typical clay court player. In an era of players hitting huge topspin shots, Tim used a variety of spins, including slice, to create opportunities to get to the net. He also made it very uncomfortable for the baseline players who like a patterned, rhythmical ball. This is a testimony to Tim being a great student of the game, but more importantly, a student of *his* game.

Most valuable of all, Tim planned out his yearly tournament schedule and training program very carefully to get the most out of his game. The British press was quite critical at times because the country had not had a male Wimbledon winner since the 1930s, when Fred Perry won Wimbledon from 1934–36. Yet Tim Henman reached the quarterfinals eight times, the semifinals four of those times—undoubtedly an incredible accomplishment.

I coached Tim for four years, from 2004–07, and it was both a pleasure and a privilege to do so. Tim was always a total professional. This does not mean he achieved every short-range goal, but his reaching No. 4 in the world was validation enough of where his talent level was.

How did he do it?

Once again, the same consistent prerequisites for success.

Tim knew exactly who he was, and where he was going.

He set appropriate goals, and followed them.

His plan was always intact, he persevered as well as any player I've ever worked with, and he never lost his absolute belief in himself. (Or his sense of humor, I might add.)

Unquestionably, Tim was a devoted athlete and his attention to detail played a major role in his achievement as a professional tennis player.

66 *The spirit, the will to win, and the will to excel are the things that endure. These qualities are so much more important than the events that occur.* **99**
– VINCE LOMBARDI

4.

The Spirit of Belief

THE EVOLUTION OF ROGER FEDERER

As we go on our life journey, the world around us changes. Nothing ever stays the same except change itself, and this is especially true in a game like tennis. When change occurs, as it often does, we might need to adjust our plans to fit the needs of the moment. One action leads to another. That law of nature defines the ball going from one side of the court to another…but add to that a high wind, sun. Add to that an unexpected play or player. One move or remove can alter an entire tournament.

I learned a crucial lesson about change during my time with Roger Federer. When I started with Roger, he was just about to turn 29 years old. But by then he'd played over 900 matches in his career. From the start, I spent a great deal of time speaking with Pierre, his strength and conditioning coach. I wanted to fully understand Pierre's philosophy of training and fitness.

Evolution, or rather adaptation, was at the heart of it. As an athlete ages he needs more rest and recovery. Hard work becomes harder. When we're younger, our body can absorb more punishment and it can recover more quickly. But as time passes the body needs more time to rebound. Pierre's insight was to manage our plan so that Roger could effectively meet the demands of his career. As a result of Pierre's expertise and timing, Roger adapted and adjusted very well. In point of fact, he did not show his age much at all.

Roger trained hard, but his remarkable ability to think things through was also extremely helpful to him. Add to that the fact he listens well and is very smart. All of these things give him an edge over many other players.

The morning I arrived in Switzerland for our first workout, Roger said, "OK, just tell me what you want to do—"

I said, "Really? It's that simple?"

He said, "Well, actually…I do like to know why I am doing what I am doing."

I smiled at his openness, his desire to listen and learn. The plan, by itself, isn't enough. He wanted to understand the point of what he is doing.

This is the thinking man's champion, I thought, and I liked that very much.

It is so logical—in order to believe in a plan, you must *understand* the plan, and *why* you are executing it.

Roger was on top of this, as he would also be on top of his game.

Roger Federer's prowess is coupled with a keen intelligence at every curve of the ball and at every stage of his career. It was Roger's mind that allowed the training, rest and recovery module to take root. Actually, he'd been doing this all along; but it had to be tempered to his present environment, his age. This is quite difficult to do when you have played so much and won so many tournaments. It's change at its most volatile and many athletes do not recover from the realization of their own maturity.

It requires a different and wiser point of view. A less-is-more philosophy. When you accept that, and understand that it's better for mind and body, it allows you to play for a longer period of time at a higher level of performance.

Pierre and I were on the same page and Roger was in stride with this as well. We are all creatures of habit, so change is not always an easy theme to grasp, especially when you are the *winningest* player in the history of the men's game. I was amazed at Roger's willingness to grasp the concept and his seamless acceptance of the plan.

Back in July of 2010, Roger and I had a great discussion about *his* game and *the* game in general. Roger loved to play, loved to travel and compete, but his results were not quite where he wanted them to be.

"The game is changing," I told Roger. "The athletes are changing and you are changing. For many people this is tough to cope with. For you it is great because now, it will be about managing your style of play and shot selection. Most people don't have the talent and versatility, the strategies and shot selection that you have, while playing at the very highest level… so this should be a lot of fun."

In Roger's most dominant years he just overwhelmed his opponents and really could play strategically almost whenever and however he wanted to.

But now his toughest competitors were coming into their prime and playing their best tennis. The thinking man's champion had work to do. We outlined the program, and went to work. Roger had bought in and *believed* in this plan of attack.

As a result, during the next four months Roger won four of eight tournaments and got to the finals of two, and the semifinals of two more. All together Roger compiled a 37-win and four-loss record, a fitting reward to a well-thought-out and cleanly executed plan.

The thing to remember as you remind yourself of your own goal is that *process changes* as players continue in their career, whatever that career may be. Nothing in life remains the same and it is good to know this when you are training for anything that matters to you, whether it is parenthood, recreational sport, business or art. It is all the same; different forms, similar practices.

When Roger was in his early to mid-20s, his body and mind worked differently. Along with this chronological change there were business responsibilities and general life changes as well—his responsibilities were of a larger and more demanding kind. This is a lot to keep in balance while playing one of the toughest one-on-one sports. Yet, in spite of these demands, Roger had become the most accomplished male player in the history of the game. And also he'd become a "global brand" and a business magnate. And a father of twins. So now you may have a better picture of his big picture.

Roger is, of course, "the given" in the equation of Team Federer and one of his greatest gifts is his clear-sightedness. His objectivity. Roger can detach himself from a situation in a unique way and thus evaluate the salient facts related to his game. Moreover, learning this way, easily and responsively, he also quickly adapts. Roger's uncanny ability to adapt to whatever is happening, whatever needs to be done, is paramount to his performance.

During the ATP Finals in London in November of 2010, Roger and I were discussing the plan for the week. He had family and friends visiting along with business meetings and I knew it would be a busy week.

I said, "It's been a terrific year and a great fall and you are playing well, so this week I think it's really important to focus on your style of play and really stay focused on how you want to approach each point of each match. Let's just try to do a good job of managing your time so you have a full tank of gas this week. It's been a long year and a lot of tennis, and activity."

Roger said, "Yeah, will do, I've been feeling good and comfortable with my game, it will be fun to be here with the other top guys and see how it goes, and the other stuff shouldn't be too draining."

"Sounds good," I told him. "We'll keep the tank full and as far as the tennis goes, on this surface, it will be important to use all of your variation to create offense and get your opponents uncomfortable."

Roger replied, "I think things will be good here and it will be fun to play the best players and use the things, the strategies we've been working on." Yes, he said it was "fun" looking forward to it, embracing the challenge and process. (Note to self: *solid mentality.*)

In London, the top eight players of the year were there to face off during the culminating event on the ATP calendar. Suffice to say, Roger was incredible and beat No. 1, 3, 4 and 5 in the world to take home the trophy.

With all the pressures of being a top performer, how does a guy like Roger turn off the world and *listen* to what's important for him to hear? How does he manage to internalize the key things that apply to him as a world class player? Is there something here we might learn from, or use ourselves?

I have noticed Roger's brilliance, his personal listening acuity—occurs because he allows himself the freedom to hear what is being said without personal judgment, without twisting it around in his mind…without getting smothered by the emotional conditions that detract from the learning process. Roger hones in on one thing—*what he must do to succeed.* His focus is therefore unvarying. His mind is on the task at hand. He will not be distracted or discouraged in any way. He will learn. He will do. He will succeed. His record shows that he has done this not once, but more times in his career than I could count.

One time I was sitting in the player's lounge during the 2011 Canada Masters with Roger. We were discussing players' evolution and emotional maturity, as we were watching Gael Monfils and Viktor Troicki on TV. At one point during the match Troicki seemed annoyed by both his tennis and some of the umpire's decisions.

I said to Roger, "It's really hard to help a player at this level if they're not able to deal with adversity and accept imperfection." Then I asked him, "How did you get your emotional balance?"

"When I was younger," he replied, "I had a big temper. At times I struggled to practice, and also when things didn't go right I would just go through the motions."

"So how did you change that—coaching? Parents? Something else?"

"Ultimately, I made the decision myself. Everyone would say how talented I was—but it took me time to just accept things—and learn to compete, regardless of how things were going that day. Coaches and people around me tried to convince me how to behave but I felt like it was up to me to decide, and live by that decision, which I did."

Then he added, "I just wanted to make sure I was professional and didn't miss out because of something I could control, like my mental approach."

This was very interesting to me because although they are very different people, a similar process occurred with Pete Sampras. Pete said to me that his turning point was the 1992 U.S. Open and his final loss to Stefan Edberg. "I didn't give everything I had… and that just ate away at me." After a short pause, Pete said, "I just made my mind up that I would not let that happen again—if I lost, so be it, just leave it out on the court and do everything possible on the day to get the most out of myself, and move on."

Moving on from there, Pete's record in Grand Slam finals was 13 wins, three losses. 16 final appearances is an amazing achievement; 13 wins of those 16, is tough to quantify with words. Best to just sit back and enjoy it, no words—it feels better like that.

Both of these champions came to quite similar conclusions. All the help in the world cannot change you unless *you* want to change *yourself.* This is something we can all learn from in whatever endeavor we are involved in—in the end it comes down to what we do ourselves with what we have been given. Our personal toolbox, so to speak.

In looking at the careers of Sampras, Henman, and Federer—not to mention a great many others—the will to succeed must coincide with the will to improve. And as the athlete gets older, this becomes even more important. It seems to me the power of belief in oneself is forged by many things, including the ability to listen and the desire to learn as we go, and keep going, and keep going.

Special to be in tennis' Cathedral with Roger.

66 *Setting a goal is not the main thing. It is deciding how you will go about achieving it and staying with that plan.* **"**

– TOM LANDRY

5.

Eight Steps
to Success

WHAT ARE YOUR GOALS AND REQUIREMENTS OF THE PROJECT?

T he importance of getting the right people on your team is paramount. And there is a fine balance between the information you may accumulate and your ability to refine it and put it to good use. Too much data can cause circuit overload before you've even begun your program.

Much of my development as a tennis player came with help from my teammates at the University of Tennessee with Coach DePalmer at the helm. Thanks Coach.

I remember in the middle of my career I was receiving some great advice from some terrific coaches. Most of them wanted me to work on my game from the back of the court and become more well rounded. I was a relentless serve and volleyer and did absolutely everything to end up at the net, even returning first serves and coming forward often. I just felt this was what I was best at, so I got to the net as soon as possible. Well, some very good coaches convinced me to work on my all-around game. I did so and my ranking plummeted 30 or 40 spots.

This frustrated me. So I consulted with my brother, Steve, who was my coach and the one who'd been with me through thick and thin.

"What do you think?" I asked. "Am I getting *worse* as I get *better?*"

"You look much better losing now," Steve said, smiling.

"What?"

"Your game is more well-rounded," Steve explained. "The points are longer and so the tennis *looks* better. Therefore, *you* look much better. The downside is you're losing."

I shook my head. "All right, what's next?"

Steve replied, "Look, let's just keep it simple and get back to basics, and win or lose while doing what you do best. Get it clear in your mind. BUT GET TO NET, AND GET THERE QUICK!"

Shortly after this great bit of advice, I ended a long drought by winning the ATP event in Vienna. It was such a relief and made me realize although there is some great knowledge out there, it's so important to keep the information clear, concise and on point.

Steve has a great sense of the game and, in particular, my game. He was my rock on tour, in tennis, life, and friendship. He always was and is the best. My deepest thanks go out to him and at the same time I pass on the fact that such a person in your life can make all the difference.

So, summing up, what you need to do is get the best people to help you meet your goal. Your team, by the way, may consist of your husband or wife, or best friend, or another person. Team is used generically here for any number beyond one.

When Pete Sampras was gearing up for his final push in the summer of 2002, we adjusted his plan, made a few tweaks, committed ourselves to the process, and got right to work.

The modus operandi was a streamlined version of something we'd discussed many times before.

This can be summed up as: assess, discuss, adapt or adjust. Then follow the plan, work the process. If that sounds simplified, it's because it is. On the other hand, the goal can be very far off, and getting to it can seem very complicated if you are not following these practical and primary steps.

Pete's application was perfect. And if ever it went astray, for any reason, we adapted and improvised to adjust to a new "environment."

It helped that he was a great player with great dedication. He also had an unvarying, fully-committed focus. The end result: the 2002 U.S. Open championship.

PUT THE RIGHT SUPPORT TEAM IN PLACE.

As I have been emphasizing, your support team is vital. There is no correct number. Every person, and every industry has different needs and different components. This will play a role in how you set up the Team. Be clear to yourself and the Team. Make sure you do the best you can to keep things streamlined and manageable. Make sure each person knows his or her role and you know how to tap into individual expertise. But teams aren't for everybody. The definition of Team can vary from person to person. Sampras would have a very hard time if he had employed Federer's multi-faceted support group. Pete required a team that was streamlined, simple and clear. He preferred and excelled in a more insular environment. Roger can manage larger groups and not get wrapped up in a larger number of people assisting. He delegates, gives autonomy, and then doesn't worry about it. He has complete faith in his choice of people to handle the tasks at hand.

Roger has a great feel for putting people in the right roles to support him and maximize his chance for success.

WHAT IS YOUR PLAN AND HOW WELL WILL IT WORK?

As you evaluate where you are, at any stage of the game, make sure you go through your key areas to develop the plan of action.

When you make a plan and then implement it, things do not always work out with seamless precision at the outset. Here is an example: in the fall of 2013 I was working with Sloane Stephens and we mapped out a good plan. Our process was thoughtfully outlined and we were ready...but let me give you a little back story.

Sloane was 20 years old. The year before, at 19, she had made a big splash by defeating Serena Williams in the Australian Open quarterfinals to reach the semifinals. But now Sloane was navigating a new landscape filled with many different elements, and perhaps some distractions, outside the game of tennis.

Her new environment, as I observed, was rife with expectation, and this, quite naturally, caused her to feel pressured. With outward pressure comes inner tension, the result of which can be readily seen in competition. This knocked Sloane off the path of her well-defined plan, and additionally, it created both frustration and doubt.

Much of our time together was spent in trying to maintain her plan while learning to trust the long term impact of her chosen path. As a young person thrust into a sudden new environment, this was a huge challenge, and many of the initial difficulties we faced together were tempered by the need to replace doubt with certainty.

To Sloane's credit, her skill and resilience carried her forward. She was able to push past these hurdles, winning three WTA titles in 2016. Since then, she has been sidelined due to foot surgery.

In November of 2003, Henman and I discussed his program and what tools we needed to use in order for his rise to excellence. We mapped out the training schedules, the areas to focus on, and how best to pursue what we might call his "competitive opportunities." Perhaps I should define this more specifically as the *style of play* that Tim needed to strive for. Once his plan was set, the rest fell into place—a disciplined daily regimen, that each day,

became a building block to achieve the stated goal of championship tennis.

In your own field, whatever it might be, get the key components lined up first. Then address whatever aspects of the design are the most critical. This way the application will be smooth and logical but also impactful. Again, this need not be a large complex design. Rather it should be thoughtful, detailed and clearly prioritized.

WHAT DOES YOUR SUPPORT TEAM THINK OF IT?

Now you are all set to get with your team and make sure you have a fully rounded debate about the effectiveness of your program. Is there unreserved belief and buy-in?

Does the team, the people you trust, believe in the inevitable success of your process? It's not enough—at this point—to imagine that they do; they need to say they do, and mean it. Absolute commitment.

Your team, one member or 100 members, will play a key role in making the plan a complete success.

WHAT IS YOUR PRESENTATION LIKE? IS IT CONVINCING?

Be as thorough as possible. Also be as passionate as possible. Be as comprehensive as possible. Do not leave any part of the process out; don't "soft pedal" any aspect of it. Keep it straight and clear. Without clarity, without total commitment, the process will be flawed; the plan will not reach the goal.

When Roger and I first discussed his desire to finish 2010 *strong,* he was clear about what he wanted to do and the way he wanted to do it. As we discussed it with Team Federer, Roger made sure our roles were clearly defined. We talked about how the process was going to unfold both *before, during* and *after* the tournaments.

As much as a team needs clarity, team members also need passion. They need to be convinced that the process makes sense—from the get-go to the triumph at the end. Passion is key, but so is logic. Therefore, you need to present this logic with passion. Passionate logic almost seems to be a contradiction, but believe me, it works.

Team members need to hear your commitment. I vividly remember Nick Bollettieri meeting with the entire academy and telling the staff and players how hard work and discipline will not only make the players the best they can be, but also make the academy the best it can be. Since those pep talks of the 1970s, the Nick Bollettieri Tennis Academy has become arguably the most prolific in the industry. For the past 30 years, Nick and his academy have developed more top 10 players than any other tennis school in the world. Excellence is not an accident… and there is passionate logic in black and white.

WHAT ARE THE SPECIFIC STEPS LEADING TO YOUR GOAL?

As I have been saying, each step in the design of the program needs to be concise and clear, and therefore, *specific*. As I was completing my college tennis career, my college coach Mike DePalmer, Sr. and my brother Steve (who was soon to be my coach on the pro tour) each gave me some valuable advice.

Coach D said, "You have to live and die by your athleticism and your ability to hurt people by getting to the net."

Steve added, "In order to do that, you need to continue to get stronger, faster, and more agile and to work on finding patterns in points that will allow you to move forward and apply pressure."

From that point on, we spent a lot of time during my last year in college working in these specific areas. Coach D was relentless in his 6:30 a.m. practice sessions. He was forcing me to push my body when I was hardly even awake. "The pain will pay off," he said.

Coach D is a completely selfless man whose many sacrifices on my behalf helped me greatly, not only as a player but also as a coach and as a person.

Anyone fortunate enough to have been coached by this man knows that his knowledge and guidance are second to none.

Our morning and afternoon workouts were about building a game that could withstand intense competition and succeed at the professional level.

I recall that sometimes I'd regress into what I call "college mode"—getting caught up in a loss, playing it and replaying it. Both Steve and Coach D replaced this incorrect habit of thinking with the big picture plan which was free of doubt and insecurity. It concentrated instead on the positive steps that we were executing. And this is what made me a pro and not just another good college player who was not going to make it on tour. I did, and I owe it to them.

Just one month out of college I qualified for Wimbledon and reached the quarterfinals beating the then-No. 12 in the world, Johan Kriek. That was the catalyst I needed to believe I could not only survive but could succeed as a professional tennis player.

We can mirror this process in our daily lives, but we must first be willing to take the right steps to secure the goal. And then we must be willing to implement them, adapt to new ones as we continue, and always be ready for unexpected challenges. One win or even several wins will not make success inevitable. Only work, talent and repeated effort will do this.

Roger making a smoke-filled entrance onto the 02 Arena in London as
17,000 fans watch the world's top eight men compete at the ATP Finals.

WHAT ADAPTATIONS ARE NECESSARY AND WHEN ARE THEY APPLIED?

When Henman needed to tweak his process in the fall of 2003, it started with a brief phone call and evaluation of where he was, where he wanted to go, and finally the adjustment of the plan and how to get there. This was a catalyst for some tremendous tennis for Tim.

We did not overhaul his complete regimen, rather we evaluated and modified based upon the current environment. The modifications were clear and manageable. There were drills and exercises to maximize volleying and offensive skills. We sought ways to take an opponent's time away from him. We kept our noses out of newspapers and media during Wimbledon. We made certain there was enough time for rest and recovery.

Tim was committed to all of these things and he adapted himself well to each new situation on the court. In short, he made himself resilient and flexible in order to reach the goal. The reward for his discipline came 12 months later when his ranking rose from No. 41 to No. 4 in the world.

WHAT IS THE BIG PICTURE PERSPECTIVE AND HOW CAN IT HELP YOU?

Whether you are starting your career, poised in mid-career or wrapping it up, as we say, your "big picture perspective" is vital. At 24, Sloane Stephens has had to manage expectation as well as the seesaw of winning and losing. This can be very challenging to one's confidence and confusing to one's psyche. Sloane is dealing with this better and better. There will be more bumps in the road and more adversity, but her focus on the big picture of how it all works in her career as a whole has allowed her some equanimity as well as the ability to focus on her evolving process. With this in mind, her progress continues right along.

Sampras didn't win a title for more than 25 months. This was subpar for someone with his variety of extraordinary skills, but he didn't let this deter him from his ultimate goal, winning one more major. Pete's recognition of the big picture perspective allowed us to plot his course without any discouragement. Missteps often lead to mistakes in thinking and then negativity creeps in and erodes confidence.

Resilience, perseverance and *big picture perspective* can assist a good work ethic and the other components of the process. Following this rigorously will keep you on track. Obviously it takes incredible discipline. Remember, when everything is going well, life is easy. But true character is tempered by adversity—and as we know, there's a lot of that in everyday life.

Why not accept it, embrace it, and use it as a positive motivation? A strong and positive *sense of inevitability* is what champions have in abundance. It's what drives them to achieve what seems to be unattainable. I think Pete would agree with this, especially after his campaign in 2002 and his ultimate win—holding up that trophy to claim his 14th Grand Slam title.

66 *Most of us serve our ideals by fits and starts. The person who makes a success of living is one who sees his goal steadily and aims for it unswervingly. That's dedication.* **99**
– CECIL B. DEMILLE

6.

From the
Bottom Up

n the game of tennis, as it is with all sports and in fact most things in life, we begin with fundamentals and then, later on, move on to the more complex issues of the game. Training is a matter of repetition until we've acquired conditioned responses that become almost like reflexes. When good habits are ingrained they become second nature. Even the best players have gone through this same process. They make it look easy. But they too made early sacrifices, learned the basic mechanics, and profited from them. Natural talent takes you only so far. After that, it's up to you. How far are you able to go?

BUILDING THE RIGHT FOUNDATION

When starting anything new, the key is getting the basics down. Pete Sampras did not wake up and just have the best second serve in the history of the game, nor did Federer's forehand just "appear." This took years of disciplined thought and practice, after which came the boilermaker of tough competition. The shots that look almost effortless on TV evolved over a period of many years.

The components of Pete and Roger's success come from the basics: learning proper technique, and making solid contact with the ball.

How is this different from daily life?

In truth, it isn't.

First day on the job, for instance, you start by learning and remembering your colleagues' names and by studying the way things are done in your new work environment. No one hits a grand slam on the first day.

It's this elementary process of skill building, one foot in front of the other, that teaches technique. Early on in tennis, the emphasis is on the physical. You have to learn how to strike the ball before discovering the way to put a spin on it. Then, given time and practice, different shots and unique techniques come into play at a higher level.

The variety of shots, slices and angles you see in a player like Roger is strategically important to his game. But not initially. Not even for him. The mechanics of tennis, the building blocks of skill, come first. Once those are understood, then it becomes easier to understand how to execute the arsenal of shots that are the signature of the skilled player.

But how can we—in any endeavor—move forward in a direct and uncomplicated way?

Well, to put it bluntly, the more variables we create for ourselves at the outset, the harder it is to execute our plan.

Repetition and well-designed drills are the answer.

Strategy?

As I've been saying, it must come later.

First the body needs to learn how to think on its own, and this can only happen when the primary skill-set— the tool box, so to say—is put in place. With proper physical mechanics, good habits grow and become basic reflexes.

Once the body has memorized the drill, then the mind can add an overall strategic plan.

In tennis, in the drilling stage, it's imperative to not only *see and hear* what you are doing well but also try to *feel* what is happening. This allows you to begin to memorize the feeling, to inculcate it. An example is the way a good solid connection with the ball feels.

In 1995, when I first started working with Pete, I remember a conversation about his running forehand. Pete had the innate skill of being almost fully stretched out on the dead run and able to hit the ball with incredible pace and accuracy. I asked him about this shot.

Pete said, "When I was younger, Robert Landsdorp, who used to work with me, would have me hit 100s and 100s of balls running side to side on the baseline. He loved to do this with all of his students once the technique of the shot was in place. I would do it until I could barely stand up. It came to the point that during a match I would merely turn and run and it all just flowed from there."

Basically Pete had hit so many shots like this it had become like a reflex; his eyes would see the ball, his rote learning would take over and his athletic skills would produce some of the most amazing running forehands anyone could imagine.

Granted Pete's incredible athletic skills and mental capabilities could make this shot look almost routine, but his preparation and skill building allowed it to blossom, just like you or I could do in any endeavor we are trying to execute.

I believe that we all have innate skills and senses and sometimes it is more effective to rely on this sense of feeling, this kinetic connection, which is more unconscious than conscious on the part of the player than it is to achieve a textbook perfect shot or stroke. The same may be said of life and the work place; certain applications produce certain results, feelings, reactions. It is important to feel these and become aware of them so that they can be encoded. Once filed, they may be used or disused in the future. But the important thing is they have been "witnessed" and later will be remembered by the body.

Later on, the power of certain moments in the game become strategic. For instance, Sampras was certainly aware that his opponents feared his serve. They had reason to be afraid, and Pete used this to his advantage.

Federer knew, and knows, that his opponents aren't overjoyed to see him line up to

rip a huge forehand.

Both Pete and Roger have used their technique to produce desirable and almost inevitable strategies, particularly in what I would call the big moments of a match.

I remember Pete serving for the match in the finals of the 2002 U.S. Open against Andre Agassi, arguably the greatest returner men's tennis has ever seen. The look in Pete's eyes was clear, confident and matter of fact. Andre, on the other hand, seemed a bit resigned to having to react rather than having control of the situation.

Why?

Was it history, reputation, fact or what?

Really, it doesn't matter.

Regardless of what it was I can say this: here on the cutting edge of a career-making, historical game was a player whose cumulative process over many years had built a power base of "feeling" that was felt, sensed, even apprehended by his opponent.

The beauty of knowing this is that we, learners in our own right at whatever we are doing in life, can do the same thing. We can practice, learn, and hone technique, while allowing our body-mind to memorize these dynamic feelings of success, so that they can be repeated time after time.

But how, you may ask, does this relate specifically to your career, your work environment, or your life, in general?

It's no different, in point of fact, than the feel of the racket in hand and the sound made by the ball when a serve connects in such a way that every sinew of the hand and arm knows the aim and trajectory are accurate.

For the same token, you know when your pep talk is connecting to your team, your organization, or colleagues. You know—or some part of you knows—exactly what that feels like, when words you've expressed hit home.

A salesperson knows in his very marrow when a raised question is answered in such a way as to make a sale. A teacher knows when a student is moved by a word, gesture, or point of view.

It is all a matter of connection. Making the right move at the right time, feeling the pulse of the moment, the drive of the ball when we hit it right.

We are all players at what we do. All games of life have rules. All actions within the

game are essentially "in" or "out." It's our job to imprint the feeling of "in" as well as the feeling of "out." When we can learn from our mistakes, triumph over them, and produce winning results, we are on the path of excellence. When we belabor our mistake, we are out. When we feel in "the groove" are we not experiencing the repetition of body moves, mind moves and memory synchronicity that places us in perfect harmony with the game of life?

66 *The will to win is nothing without the will to prepare.* **"**
- JUMA IKANGAA

7.

Hot Shots

Kids naturally want to play, so the question for us, as adult sponsors, teachers and parents is not only how do we make it fun for them but also how do we manage to keep them there—playing for fun but also to learn? Well, there is a way to let kids play, learn, and stay in the game, hopefully, for life. It's called Tennis Hot Shots and it was developed by Tennis Australia. The way it works is that through this unique system, players under 12 learn the game faster and more enjoyably than in years past when it was common to teach children as if they were just adults.

Founded in 2008, Tennis Hot Shots is based on the idea that kids learn more quickly when they serve, rally and play with the appropriate size racquet, court and low compression ball, while also being encouraged by the right kind of motivation. Of course teaching the basic technique of strokes is still emphasized, but standing in a line waiting for a turn is not. Inactivity, in general, is one of the primary causes of lack of attention—the real killer of young interest in any sport.

Since financial institution ANZ announced its sponsorship of the program in 2014, Tennis Hot Shots has significantly increased junior tennis participation in Australia. For example, more than 500,000 children have experienced ANZ Tennis Hot Shots in the last 12 months alone, and the program is being delivered to more than 5,000 venues in Australia.

As we have emphasized here, at the core of Hot Shots is the innovative, practical philosophy of *learning through play*. Playing the game of tennis, or modified versions of the game, is the focus of all sessions, and it is the reason why children stick with it. We all like to "play" but children, even more than adults, need to play to learn the rigor of the game.

Using tailored equipment, including smaller courts, racquets and low-compression tennis balls, kids are introduced to tennis in an environment well-suited to their age, skill and mental proclivity. There is nothing hard to understand about this—such an approach makes learning tennis fun and easy, and at the same time, it allows more children to play at a higher level and better standard. It also effectively encourages kids to play tennis more often. By making *desire* to play commensurate with *will* to play, there is a balance that is always present. An observer can readily see technical and tactical competence grow as desire to play is actively present. The idea is this: "I *want* to play" is supported by "I will learn *how* to

play." Together these two concepts re-affirm the age-old principle of "This is fun!"

How is the "fun principle" augmented on a daily teaching level? The Hot Shots initiative essentially has four pillars of learning: schools, coaching, community activity and leagues. All four, working in harmony with young people, become a total learning experience rather than an isolated, non-integrated one.

Once children have been introduced to the sport through school and have learned the fundamentals of the game through coaching programs, it is critical to transition them into team-based competition. The transition to playing the game with a team of friends enables children to put their skills into practice and develop a love of the game that will keep them playing tennis well into the future. Team-based competition is key to developing future tennis champions, as children acquire greater tactical awareness and technical proficiency.

As a coach and a former young player myself, I can attest to the need for building a user-friendly environment for youth-oriented tennis instruction. By building a nourishing foundation that includes mental as well as physical skills, coaches can focus on proper swing patterns for their players at a very young age. Racquet size, weight, court size, and ball bounce are all important here.

When, for example, racquets are shorter and lighter, kids do not develop what might be called "extreme grips." As a result, one-handed backhands are more common in this program. Arguably, there is more chance to implement varied tactics and strategies when the young player isn't over-challenged by a heavy, adult-type racquet. Who knows, we may yet see net-rushing as a more common occurrence at the professional level down the road. I certainly believe it's possible.

For the health of the sport in the future, we must have an emphasis on kids playing tennis and developing a love of the game all around the world. Kids have so many choices today. And there is social motivation to do so many other things, especially in the area of video games and social media. Based on this challenge, the teacher or coach has to meet students' needs in a unique way. If we do this the Hot Shots way, I believe we will also ensure that tennis stays

relevant into the next generation. It is a given that today's kids are our future participants, champions and fans, and most importantly, our future leaders.

66 *The main thing is to stick with the positive.* **99**
- PAUL ANNACONE

8.

Moving Forward
Without Stress

Many countries have now started to embrace the Hot Shots concept if not the actual program itself. Players such as Justine Henin, Kim Clijsters and Federer, to name a few, spent time in their early years learning tennis with modified equipment and in the spirit of Federer's priceless and memorable remark—"Slower balls, smaller court... easy game!"

Even Roger's effortless rhythm and accuracy need fine tuning.

What this says to me is that we need the right tools to maintain and sustain interest. But there also needs to be an appropriate level of accomplishment, so that young players can move forward more quickly and with less internal stress.

A player who is continually frustrated by the tools of the game will most likely become disheartened. This brings on the old model of diminishing returns which, incidentally, exists to some extent in all sports training at the beginning level. Coaches, consciously or unconsciously, help to bring this about when they create rigor without the accompanying joy of vigor.

I believe the main thing is to stick with the positive. Or said another way—stick with what works. Generally, what works best, in my experience, is not being blindly discouraged before you even have a feel for the ball. And even once you have that "feel for the ball" later on, it is necessary to hold to the optimistic view—everything's going to be OK if I keep my focus and continue to feel that the game is both fun and challenging at the same time.

As I've been saying, learning tennis skills is not all that different from learning any techniques that fit into the game of life. The same consciousness cited above will enhance someone coming into a new work environment. Why make it harder for them? Why challenge them beyond their initial need to be challenged? Sometimes change itself is a large enough challenge in life.

All of us, no matter what we're doing to make a living, have a certain innate talent, a skill in a particular area of endeavor. I wonder though how many of us realize that the most important skill of all is dedication toward improvement. Let's take a look at some common ground.

You may be familiar with the research of Dr. K. Anders Ericsson. Dr. Ericsson is a psychologist at Florida State University who has performed extensive research with talented individuals. In particular, he has looked at what makes top level athletes and musicians successful. His findings are quite clear in that "deliberate practice," as he calls it, is the most important attribute to reaching expertise in a specific field. To be more specific, it takes approximately 10 years or 10,000 hours of total commitment to become an expert at something.

As it turns out, innate talent is less important than intensive effort, focus and practice. This is clear in the sport of tennis as well. There is no substitute for practicing forehands, backhands and serves while focusing on proper form and technique. The questions you need to ask in your specific area of activity are the following: What are the things I need to do to reach the next level? Am I practicing these important skills often enough? Equally important, how can I measure my improvement, and make sure I am carrying out each skill properly?

As young players improve however, they have to find a path for that progression. They need to be able to move up to bigger rackets and courts as needed based on their skill improvement. Do you have a clearly laid out plan for progress? This should be a plan to improve your own skills without attaching yourself to how many promotions you might get as a result. Actually, if you focus on improving your skills, beneficial things will happen to you as a matter of course. In general, make yourself indispensable by learning a variety of skills that can be used in different situations. In other words, like Roger, be versatile!

Whether you are playing tennis, or coaching, or perhaps just trying to improve your business model, you will need the same program I am talking about. You need to be excited and anticipatory about your work. You can't go through the motions and expect magic to happen. You must be fully engaged each day.

One way to do this is to ask yourself why you are working on whatever specific project you have elected to do. What is the big picture, the wide-angle scope?

Are you taking pride in your work? Or are you just doing it? By caring deeply about your work, you will find yourself more focused on exactly what that work is. Many of us work blindly, as if the work itself was a deliverance of some kind. Well, to some it may be just that. But to many the enjoyment factor lessens as the repetition increases. It shouldn't be that way; it should be the opposite.

I like to make a checklist for each plan or project that I undertake. For me, this is like a carpenter choosing the right tools. If you don't have the right tools, how are you going to succeed? In business the right tools may be any or all of the following: information, documents, contacts, or equipment. The journey toward success becomes a whole lot easier when you have particularized your needs fulfillment and capitalized on the tools that are necessary for completion.

This idea fits in closely with "keeping it interesting." Most people who move up in an organization are those who recognize the big picture right from the start. Tennis players such as Federer and Sampras both have a keen understanding of the history of the sport and what it takes to become a part of that history.

In your activity, whatever it may be, ask yourself how your part works in congruence with the whole picture. Where does your department, your personal skill, fit in? What can you do to make yourself indispensable rather than merely auxiliary? How can you help others to function in a similar and harmonious way?

These are important questions to ask yourself—not just once in a while—but on a regular basis. Asking will help you keep your focus and your plan in good order.

To facilitate your process, here are five steps you can take to improve your ratio of success.

STEP ONE:

Are you committed to putting in the time it might take to learn the skills necessary and/or commit to the time it might take to complete the project? List your project name and try to project how much time per day you will have to commit to reach your goal.

STEP TWO:

List the different progressions of the project. In other words, break the project down into bite-sized pieces.

STEP THREE:

How will you complete the project without it becoming monotonous? Make up a schedule that includes some variety of different tasks. Show how you will handle adversity or unexpected situations.

STEP FOUR:

Do you have all of the proper contacts, equipment and other necessary tools to complete each step of the project? Make a list and identify your needs.

STEP FIVE:

Double check that you will accomplish what you set out to do and that you will have check points along the way to make sure you are focused on the big picture. Key words, or, cues, can be very helpful here.

. . . .

Maybe some of what I'm saying sounds a bit daunting. It isn't really but it may seem so. Most large goals seem overwhelming at first. However, once you look at all the pieces of the puzzle, you may see what is lacking and what is not. Then, by building a strong foundation, you may be able to see your daily routine and chart how it happens, when it happens, and why it is happening. The key ingredient here is seeing all the parts, understanding how they fit together, and channeling all of it into a harmonious whole that works for you and everyone else.

I use tennis as a metaphor because it works as one. For instance, professional tennis players must learn all the proper techniques to hit the ball. But they must also learn how to play, how to strategize, how to compete, and ultimately, how to win matches. Actually, the business world, or any other world of endeavor in life, is no different. You must learn the basics, the necessary skills, and then you can progress toward the desired, result-oriented goal, which of course, like the tennis player, is about winning. Self-assessment will serve as a summary of each of the steps involved. If you stick with your plan, build a good foundation and don't lose sight of the big picture, you will be in a good place to see your progress. And that is where self-assessment is so important. It tells you categorically how well you're doing. With all these things in place, you will make steady progress.

In 2007, when I was head coach of men's tennis for The Lawn Tennis Association, I saw a great example of this. I was on court with a very talented young player and we were going through a training session where there was a lot of drilling and repetition. I was so impressed with the young player's ball striking, stroke production and athleticism that I wondered… *why is this kid not winning more?*

The next week I saw him start the match fine, but then 15 minutes into the match, a poor shot selection was followed up with anger and frustration, leading to a quick defeat for the young man.

I asked him after the match what he thought had happened, and he said, "I was just missing so much… I had no feel on my forehand and the ball was flying everywhere."

In and of itself this made sense and was true. But as a coach, I wanted to know more. So I said, "OK, so why didn't you adjust?"

He shook his head. "I couldn't. I was just so frustrated, I had no control, and it just went from bad to worse."

I was thinking—*This is where the mind leads the body. He created an environment where he did not allow himself to problem solve. Just 15 minutes into the match and the emotional negativity and doubt had already drained his fuel tank of optimism. He'd lost his belief in himself, and all those long hours of physical work were lost to him because of his attitude. He had the body's code integrated into a success pattern of moves but he couldn't get to them, and even worse, he couldn't get them to work for him even though his body knew exactly what to do.*

So he was willing to do the physical work of drilling and hitting the correct shot with great technique and executing it to perfection, but when the competitive aspect came into play, he was up against a personal wall of doubt. His perceived set of expectations and what-ifs were dominating his game. As a matter of course, his process just fell apart. The long hours of repetition had been logged-in, the great work of physically hitting the ball was there, encoded in his psyche, but all of it went out the window in self-doubt.

There are many ingredients to make a complete player regardless of the game. This young man's challenge was now of a different order than earlier. Now he needed to ask himself the following questions.

How good is my average level?

How well can I deal with things when they're not going smoothly on court?

How can I adjust and remain totally positive?

How can I strategize while I am in motion on the court?"

To all of these questions there are logical answers.

The most primary answer of all is to be able to see yourself objectively. Without that clarity, you can't possibly address the problem of what to do when things aren't going your way.

As a coach, I often counsel that the next thing you've got to manage is the "frustration factor." This can completely turn a match upside down for a player who is, or was, in control.

When you miss a shot, you need to ask yourself immediately—*"Did I choose the right shot?"*

If, in fact, you did, then you must ask—*was it just not great execution?*

Again, coaching brings out the technique adjustments, the execution of the perfect, or near-perfect shot.

But in action, in the heat of the match, you have to be able to think on your feet. And your body, in a sense, must also do the thinking, which is why I keep stressing the positive value of repetition. Get your bodywork down so smooth that, if your mind can't manage, your body will, and then, your next move will incorporate the necessary adjustment. This is the difference between being frustrated, angry and losing, and, on the other hand, adapting, adjusting, and winning.

66 *Sport is not about being wrapped up in cotton wool. Sport is about adapting to the unexpected and being able to modify plans at the last minute. Sport, like all life, is about taking risks.* **"**
- SIR ROGER BANNISTER

9.

Great Expectations

ADAPT AND ADJUST

When we have great expectations, we are engaging in optimism. Dreams are made of such stuff. But when we have unrealistic expectations, we are heading down the wrong track. There is a way to determine which is which. And there is a way to be on your toes, while being able to adapt realistically to change. This course of action brings the best results because it enables you to play your best, given who you are and what you wish to accomplish. Once again, I'm reminded of Sampras and his June 2000 pursuit of his 13th Grand Slam title at Wimbledon.

Top left: At 2000 Wimbledon, Pete dealt with the adversity of a debilitating shin injury and captured his seventh Wimbledon title, bringing his total number of major titles to 13. At the time, it was the most in men's tennis history.

During Pete's second round match, he felt something in his shin. After the match he was in a lot of pain and even had difficulty walking. After multiple visits to doctors, we found that Pete had damaged the protective sheath that surrounds the tendon. This is what allows you to push off on the foot, and get up on the balls of your feet. It's also what permits you to move on your feet at all.

The doctors concurred that if Pete could tolerate the pain he would not do "long-term" damage to himself and his injury would recover during the break Pete had scheduled after Wimbledon.

Pete's initial response was: "I can deal with pain, but if I can't walk, how am I going to play?"

This was going to take some serious adjusting and adapting!

We discussed numerous possibilities but decided the best plan was to listen to the tournament doctors who advised to get the shin area injected with a painkiller, prior to the matches. Between matches, nothing but rest. This would keep the use of the tendon to a minimum, and allow for some recovery during inaction. So our idea was not to practice on days between each match and no warm ups the day of the matches. We agreed to evaluate each day and adjust accordingly.

Pete was more than willing, but he still had this nagging question: "I am here to win this tournament… how can I do it in this condition?"

"You don't know what you can, or can't, do until the matches start, and you are on court," I told him. "If you can't play, you can't play. But let's not make any pre-judgments. Let's just be ready each morning. Then we'll evaluate and see what you can do."

The final piece of the puzzle was weighing in who he was—Pete Sampras, winner of six Wimbledon titles. This would play a significant role both in Pete's mind and anyone who was attempting to defeat him.

I remember the tension and anxiety as if it were only moments ago. Pete desperately wanted to win this tournament and break the men's record of 12 total Grand Slam singles titles. As I said, he'd won Wimbledon before and, to him, the place was "home." But he didn't know if he could get through this grueling ordeal and still have a chance of winning.

Get through it? Maybe.

Win it? That was the question.

Given who Pete was, a man with an extraordinary tolerance for discomfort and even outright pain, he had more than a chance. Yet with an adjusted game plan and modified mind set, I told myself, *If anyone can achieve this, Pete can.*

So then we talked strategy. Shorter points, more aggressive returning and also more aggressive serving than normal. There were other adjustments as well, but much of our conversation was about accepting what "was." Deal with what you can control, adjust as best you can, and see what happens. And I emphasized: *Let the mind help lead the body to what you can do, not what you can't.*

After losing the first set Pete went out and won the next three sets in his third round match against Justin Gimelstob. I thought this was a terrific effort, but he came off the court in significant pain, and had doubts about his ability to complete the event. He was struggling to walk.

We stuck to the routine and he got treatment after the match, then literally sat on the couch at home for a day and a half until it was time to go to the courts for the fourth round.

He was able to get through the fourth round, then the quarterfinals, then the semifinals by doing the same routine. This was truly a Herculean effort.

After winning his semifinals match we had a long talk about preparations for the final. He was to play Pat Rafter, a terrific grass court player who'd beaten Agassi in the other semifinal.

We agreed that Pete should try to hit a few balls on the off day only to get a little rhythm and to test if it was going to be possible for him to play the final without injecting the injured area.

Well, we found out very quickly—there was no way could he play without the injection, and the hit lasted about 20 minutes—because it was too painful. The 20-minute practice session was shorter than normal for an off day, but it was 20 minutes more than he'd been able to do on any other off day during the tournament. The pain was prohibitive, so Pete really did no movements, but did get to use the arm and get a little rhythm, which I believe served his mind by loosening him up a bit.

All things considered, Pete was as well prepared as possible for the final. I think by this point he was so sick of hearing my motivational clichés that he was probably ready to send me home on the next plane!

Anyway, the plans were made, and the stage was set. The players marched to the Cathedral, Wimbledon's Centre Court. There's no place quite like it on the planet.

The aura of Centre Court is numbing. When people say, "deafening silence" I always think of that prescient moment when the referee asks, "Players ready? Play!"

But, this was Pete, and this was his home. No deafening silence, no numbness, no injury, no opponent—just Pete and a plan. Just Pete and a tennis racket, a ball, and targets to hit. Confident, clear, committed and resolute in his ability to do what he'd always done, what he could do, what he would do—play tennis on *his* terms.

Rafter did a great job winning the first set in a tie-breaker and was up four points to one in the second-set tie-breaker. Then a crack in the armor, a relatively easy missed forehand passing shot by Rafter that would have all but solidified a two-set lead, a huge mountain for Pete to climb.

In the narrow margins that define levels of greatness, it still amazes me what the best can do when even a fraction of chance is presented. As I see it, Pete treated any narrow margin as if it were a Grand Canyon of opportunity.

So, with that untimely miss by Rafter, Pete won the second set tie-breaker and with a fist pump and adrenaline rush, it was now Pete's moment. He felt the momentum shift, and knew this was his chance.

However, remember what I was saying about adjustment? Although Pete was even in the match, and confident with his situation now, England's weather gods had different plans. In the heat of battle, a rain delay fell upon the two warriors.

Now a new obstacle…

The pain-killing injections were wearing off, and darkness was just around the corner.

How to proceed?

More injections?

Not recommended by the doctor.

More questions: Would the rain delay the match until tomorrow? How would the leg respond, one more time? Each day it was more difficult to physically and emotionally prepare and play. The mind and body were saying, "Enough, go home, get on the couch, get healed, decompress and take a breath."

Too many thoughts, too many distractions.

Time to get back to work, back to the plan, back to the moment. Back to the place where there's no distractions, no mind clutter. Just the goal, the mission, the plan, the champion's way—a clear mind. Play the next point, time and time again. Win or lose on your own terms, and then move on.

With the light fading and the pain level rising, Pete served out the fourth set to win the match, breaking Roy Emerson's record of 12 Grand Slam singles titles.

. . . .

2000 Wimbledon title No. 7. Pete raises his arms in euphoric, semi-disbelief after accomplishing something that 10 days prior seemed to be a pipe dream. Great expectations realized; you should never underestimate the heart and abilities of a champion.

66

Today, looking back, I feel this accomplishment was a testimony to Pete's ability to adapt and adjust. He was aided in this by his mental fortitude, the fact he believed he could create an environment where he would be successful. Facing all of his limitations, he felt no debilitating discouragement. Racket in hand, eye on the ball, Pete did a most singular thing—he played his own match, not somebody else's.

No doubt, the mind leads the body.

And when you adjust, adapt, and perform, you can really say *"Mission accomplished,"* at the end of the day.

Although media glamour, romance and history point to the result of Pete winning the tournament, and make this the primary focus of our attention, in reality, as a coach, I look back at his ability to see the conditions surrounding the nearly insurmountable task at hand, and turning it, almost magically, to his advantage. Many will say—and they're right in doing so—that it was "Pete Sampras" who made this tremendous accomplishment become a reality. I agree. But I think all of us can learn from his challenge, and take something from it to better ourselves.

The lesson Pete learned is clear to me. Tough environment, hard challenge, a mountain of adversity…and the pivotal, if undesirable, question, "What do I need to do to give myself a chance?"

It seems so clear, it seems so simple when looking at the process involved. Unfortunately, we all have so much invested in what we are doing that it's often difficult to see through the screen of emotion and drama that adversity creates all by itself. Yes, it's very difficult to weigh the task and just simply say, "Here's what I need to do…" and then do it.

It's easier, in fact, to fall into the drama of the scenario, the human emotional drain. The justification that you've been unjustly thrown a nasty curveball.

But all of this is normal, it's just life. The unexpected curveball is as much a part of life as the gleaming trophy sitting in the sun.

But what can we do to overcome when the odds are totally against us? Take a page from Pete's book. Clear your mind. Adjust, adapt and, most of all, see what happens. Your bright chance may be there inviting you to win in the worst of weathers, and when that happens great expectations trump adverse conditions.

66 *Know your limits, but never stop trying to exceed them.* **"**
– ANONYMOUS

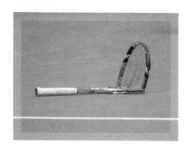

10.

Unreasonable Expectations

D reams and goals can be scary. The harsh reality of what we can and can't do is not only sobering but also stifling if we're not taking stock of the situation wisely and carefully.

Someone once told me, "If you want to make God laugh, tell him your plans."

Brilliant, and true. No matter your religious affiliation or spiritual attunement—you have to, as they say in Boy Scouts—"Be Prepared."

Life is one curveball after another. In sports, it happens even more so. The brutal reality of most sports is that in terms of results, there's really no "subjective evaluation. "There's no "on the one hand," and, "on the other hand." You just look at the score…did you win or lose? It's that simple. This can be an absolute sledgehammer when it comes to confidence. But it can also pump you up to a new level of performance. And it all depends on where you are in the win–loss column.

Dr. Noel Blundell was an invaluable resource in helping me learn how to deal with pressure and self-imposed unreasonable expectations.

Life, in general, is not much different, except for the subjective evaluations that qualify what we do. In a way, there's generally more room for the average person to say "good news and bad news" in terms of an evaluation. In sports, the reality is no one can really afford to lose without coming back and winning big time. In life, people can often lose time and again and not be noticed or judged as a complete, or even partial, failure. Perhaps this is part perception, part reality, but the bottom line is in sports you tend to live more under the microscope of the win-loss column and it's more difficult to hide. In the private sector, even if the performance is not up to par, it does not feel as "public" or as much of an open criticism, like being naked in front of a large group.

Given this kind of reality, isn't it really important in any endeavor to make your expectations reasonable and realistic? In striving for excellence, we need to remember that there are many steps along the way.

I recall my initial press conference when I started my tenure with the Lawn Tennis Association in November of 2007. I was asked right from the start: "What is your plan to alter the current path of the players? How will you help them to reach higher?"

My answer was simply, "There are no magic pills or potions. It's pretty simple. First, we need some time, a deeper talent pool, plus good coaching and development plans for the players. In addition, we need to get the players and coaches to understand the big picture and the long term goals. This doesn't happen overnight, as you know. We will need time to restructure, time to deepen that talent pool, and more time to let the process unfold."

The questions came and I answered them, and I thought things went pretty well. In fact, I generally enjoyed the discussions and questions. And I believed that the press got my message: that this was a long term process, not a quick fix. Also that, at the outset, we were merely embarking on the initial phase of a long-term plan.

Wimbledon rolled around roughly six months later with no good male results except for Andy Murray. The bashing of the players, coaches, programs, and planning was already underway. This is where unreasonable expectations kicked in. There was no possible way that after only six short months we were going to correct problems that had been going on for years. Further, we weren't about to see substantive changes at Wimbledon. This was of course the pinnacle of professional tennis and it would not be the first place of incremental change in the overall developmental plan. It would be the absolute last place where you would see the impact of "a plan" or "the plan." One might see incremental change in three to five years and, hopefully, substantive positive change in seven to 10 years. But six months? This was a case of very unreasonable expectations.

The reason I use this as an example is that it's exactly what happens in human nature whenever you set unreasonable goals in a short time span. All you're doing then is setting yourself up for failure and an emotional pummeling.

Whether you are a tennis player or information technology executive, an elementary school teacher, or a hard-working mom or dad, you must have a reasonable set of expectations. You need expectations to be attainable but also progressive. If you set your sights too high, if you make things too lofty for yourself, you will crush the desire to continue. At the first quarter mile-marker, you'll want to quit to save yourself from abject failure later on.

During one of the indoor swings with Pete Sampras in the mid-1990s, we were in Europe and Pete was practicing with someone and the guy tried to make a crazy shot. He missed and Pete looked at me and said, "A man's gotta know his limitations." He stole that line from a Clint Eastwood movie but it was very funny in this context, and we talked about it afterwards. Pete elaborated: "It's really important to know what you can and can't do. Once you've got this down, then you can make realistic goals and set up a plan where your progress can be checked, measured and achieved."

I asked him, "What about you as a kid…what were your goals and dreams like then? What were your expectations?"

"I was around people who were helping me and they were always saying how much talent I had and how great I was going to be, so I figured if I kept working hard, I would do really well."

Hard work, help, and plenty of support and confidence from those we love and trust—naturally, that is a winning combination.

Looking back, I believe Pete was stating that even as a youngster he had realistic expectations for himself—but ultimately—and this is very important— he believed in the people around him. This conditioning helped him to work harder, and then, in time, to see the results of that intensity of focus. Good things are bound to happen when you trust those around you and believe in yourself.

But…this does not mean that even for Pete everything was rosy and easy. When I first met Pete as teenager, he was just starting out on tour. There was a lot of hype, a lot of expectation thrown his way. This took some getting used to. He also happened to come along at the same time as fellow Americans Michael Chang, Andre Agassi and Jim Courier. This combined with the fact that the John McEnroe/ Jimmy Connors era in American tennis was winding down, added to the pressure of expectation.

Playing for and with teammates was a great ingredient that helped me mature.

In 1989, prior to the start of Wimbledon, Pete was visiting with his brother and we were in my apartment talking about his start on the tour and what was happening. Pete was doing well and making solid progress up the ranks but had not made the huge breakthrough of winning a Grand Slam yet. Chang had won the French Open and Agassi was already in the top 10 in the world, so Pete was a bit frustrated that he did not have that breakthrough yet.

This is a great example of where a certain environment sets the stage for unreasonable expectations. (At least, with regard to the timeline.) I told Pete that with his style of play and his versatility, it might take a little while longer to develop to the top level than for someone who is more of a one-dimensional player, like a Chang or even Agassi, for that matter. The shot selection and variety that Pete possessed took some serious management skills and maturity to fully flourish, whereas someone like Chang had a steel will and immense foot-speed, but he didn't have the complexity of shot choice, and, in actuality, it was "easier" for him to "just play."

I suggested to Pete that he should be patient with his great talent, and keep working hard. "In time it will come," I said.

We were just friends, I was merely passing on my thoughts as a friend and fellow competitor, not as a coach, which of course I wasn't at that time. Needless to say, Pete came into his own at just the right time for him—and for tennis as well.

However, this could have taken a different turn. There might've been a scenario where Pete's expectations could have hurt him, held him back or just caused him a lot of frustration. He saw his peers doing very well and he felt like he was on their level, yet he was not making the jump in the rankings like he wanted to. This could've had an ill effect on him.

But instead of wallowing in "what ifs" Pete got back to work, played each match and held to the belief that good things would come as he was told all during his crucial years as a child and younger player.

Being part of a team at the University of Tennessee helped me understand and manage my expectations.

The lesson here is that even if we do have unreasonable expectations, and even if the plan isn't working out on our timeline, you can still be a winner if you wait and be patient, and keep working while allowing for realistic and reasonable goals. As you progress, you evaluate and see where you are.

Always remember, too, that if you want to make God laugh, tell him your plans, and especially your timeline!

66 *We are all inventors, each sailing out on a voyage of discovery, guided each by a private chart of which there is no duplicate. The world is all gates, all opportunities.* **99**
– RALPH WALDO EMERSON

11

The Magician and
the Mechanic

M agic may be explained as a mysterious power or phenomenon which defies analysis or explanation. This "magic" comes to mind when watching a classic match of McEnroe's, or more recently, a live match of Federer's where his athletic skills, graceful moves, and well-balanced shots from impossible positions leave us in a state of wonderment. How could anyone have such a deft touch?

Well, McEnroe, Sampras, and Federer are the true magicians of the sport. With them and so many others there is a certain alchemy of movement, a kind of unsurpassable elegance of form.

However, there have also been great tennis players who seem to lack what most textbooks portray as "classical form." These are players of very high quality who've handled pressure well due to the high level of shot repetition executed in practice after practice. Such players have their moves almost ingrained on the competitive match court.

Lendl was more of a mechanic, relentlessly exhausting all resources to maximize his talent, and a great champion whose will drove him to the top of the game.

This repetition, combined with an incredible amount of focus and determination (and not to mention endurance), has helped these types of players develop tremendous self-confidence. Rafael Nadal, although possessing superb athletic talent, falls more into the category of being a "mechanic," a skilled artisan who nonetheless is more of a workman than a magician. This does not mean he is not a very gifted athlete, it merely means that his physical and mental nature fall into a category which is more workmanlike.

LENDL AND MCENROE

I certainly have some first-hand experience playing against Ivan Lendl (mechanic) and McEnroe (magician). Lendl could (and would) absolutely wear you down in a match. His physical play was meant to intimidate his opponents and because Ivan knew he was fitter than just about every other opponent, he could outlast you. At his best, he hit the ball harder than other players and he could keep this up for the full length of a match. John, on the other hand, often had to feel his way into a match, although, as most tennis fans know, he also had a way of intimidating his opponents. In my very first match against John, I was leading 6-4, 4-1 with a breakpoint to go ahead 5-1. At that point, John hit an incredible, and, yes, magical, half-volley that all of a sudden seemed to refocus him, because he was able to raise his game significantly. He ended up beating me 6-1 in the third set. Of course, the battles Ivan and John had against each other are legendary. The most famous is probably the 1984 French Open final where John played an astonishing first two sets only to lose to Ivan in an epic five-set battle.

COURIER AND SAMPRAS

Jim Courier, who dominated the tour in 1991 and '92, is also a great example of the mechanic type of player. His technique is not one that you'd highlight as textbook tennis but he was extremely rigorous in his preparation and discipline, which enabled him to handle pressure exceedingly well. He is a true example of a mechanic whose commitment to practicing his personal stroke production allowed him to maintain the highest level of performance.

In contrast, Sampras, is more of a magician. His innate skills and talent allowed him to feel prepared and confident without as much technical work or repetition as Courier. If Pete's environment felt right, he could come up with almost any shot. It wasn't just preparation that gave him this ability, so much as preparation with a "feeling" or a "sense" that gave him extraordinary confidence.

Now, the tricky part is recognizing and being aware of these differences. If Jim had prepared like Pete, he wouldn't have been as productive or successful in his tennis career. If Pete prepared like Jim, his artistic or magician-side would likely have burnt out. So, for each of these individuals, it was important to recognize what they needed to do for *themselves* to give them the greatest chance of reaching their potential. It's important to realize that each player is a little bit of both; Pete clearly put in countless training hours, particularly when he was younger, to hone his skills and build a terrific technical foundation. And, let's face it, Jim could hit some amazingly creative shots at times. But, bottom line, Pete is just more of a magician and Jim is more of a mechanic. This distinction is not about comparing the two, but rather being aware of the difference, and learning how to bring the best out of yourself, in anything you choose to do. We all have skills that might lead us to believe we are mechanics. On the other hand, we might never have gone so far as to cultivate or recognize the magician at work. No matter the type of skill, most people tend to lean more towards one way or the other, which is to say, towards one end of the spectrum or the opposite end.

SANTORO, THE MAGICIAN

Interestingly, there's a recently retired French player named Fabrice Santoro, who holds the record for most appearances in Grand Slam singles matches, with 70 over the course of his 17-year career! This is unheard of in the sport of tennis due to the level of competition as well as the wear-and-tear on the body. Many industry insiders have referred to Fabrice as the "magician."

But what made him successful?

By most accounts, his style was a bit awkward. He used slice forehands and backhands when others would focus on heavy topspin shots, and used two hands for both forehand and backhand strokes. This was clearly very unorthodox. However, he could hit terrific touch shots, drop shots, and lobs and could change the pace of his opponent's shot as well as anyone. The point for us to understand is that Fabrice was not a follower. He was successful within his own strengths, which were not necessarily the same as other players' strengths. He kept his opponents off balance by playing his own style.

Fabrice's ongoing alchemy was spontaneous and relentless. And I've often reflected that such a style might apply to almost any effort in life. It certainly translates well in the business world. The magician's approach—as director, CEO, or chief bottle-washer—is nothing if not creative. And those who possess such ideas, also encourage them in others. "That's not the way we do things around here" is an initiative killer. Rather, the magician turns it around, and makes it positive with, "That's new, let's try it."

The "magician-in-chief" isn't threatened by the unorthodox. He is interested to see how it will work. For every idea that doesn't pan out there are two more larger ones that will.

For the same token, a company that is comfortable sharing unique ideas, inventions, and brainstorms is going to find ways of doing things that haven't been tried before. Some of them are going to work, and work better than anyone could ever imagine. Hence, a man like Steve Jobs and a company like Apple. Make sure, your staff believes in the motto—"No idea is a bad idea." That's the Fabrice approach: try it, if it works, work it! Some guidelines for this kind of optimistic and experimental thinking are below:

THINK OUTSIDE THE BOX

PROMOTE CREATIVITY IN THE WORKPLACE

LISTEN TO NEW IDEAS WITH AN OPEN MIND

SET UP BRAINSTORMING SESSIONS

DO THE ABOVE NOT ONLY WITH OTHERS BUT WITH YOURSELF

What other lessons can be learned from outstanding tennis players? It's not as easy as saying that serve and volleyers are more aggressive in their game and in their personalities and that baseliners are more passive. In fact, both Pete and I were serve and volleyers, yet neither one of us has, or had, a particularly aggressive nature.

However, there are characteristics that help define your style, whether it's playing tennis or while doing another activity.. First of all, it's important to assess your own personality traits realistically. How do you go after the things you want? How do you behave when your latest try at something does not work as you'd imagined? How do you turn your game around on a dime and leave what didn't work behind, while forging ahead with something new?

At the end of this chapter, there are some thoughtful questions that may help determine which category you fall into: magician or mechanic, or perhaps a little bit of both. Each of us tackles challenges differently. Knowing the way you work best as an individual makes it easier to determine your particular game plan.

We must realize that this is a spectrum, a long line, and we all fit along that line *somewhere*. We need not be extreme in one category or another, but we must know ourselves to figure out our process in the pursuit of our goals.

HOW TO TELL WHO YOU ARE AND WHERE YOU FIT INTO THE PROCESS

Here is a thumbnail exploration of the archetypes of these two types of players. They are people you see in the workforce and in any field of endeavor.

MECHANIC

1. PLANS, ORGANIZES AND STRUCTURES

2. NEVER GIVES UP BECAUSE HARD WORK PAYS OFF

3. PRACTICES REPETITIVELY

4. PUTS AN EMPHASIS ON DISCIPLINE, DETAIL, AND STRUCTURE

5. FOCUSES MORE ON TASK AND PROCESS THAN THE ENVIRONMENT THAT CONTAINS THEM

MAGICIAN

1. GETS A FEEL FOR THE OVERALL PROJECT OR TASK

2. WORKS AT THE MOST OPTIMAL TIME

3. HAS CONFIDENCE IN STAYING WITH AN IDEA OR PROJECT BECAUSE SOMETHING MIGHT ALL OF A SUDDEN CLICK

4. USES VARIETY AND SPONTANEITY AS TOOLS

5. EXPERIENCES THE SURROUNDING ENVIRONMENT AND USES THIS KNOWLEDGE TO AN ADVANTAGE

WHEN IS A WIZARD JUST A MAN WITH A GOAL?

John Wooden was sometimes called the "Wizard of Westwood." Widely recognized as one of the greatest coaches of all time, Coach Wooden was the men's basketball coach at UCLA for 27 years where he led the basketball team to become a dynasty, winning 10 NCAA National Championships (including seven in a row). Thinking about mechanics and magicians made me think of Coach Wooden, especially because his nickname was the "Wizard of Westwood."

But was Coach Wooden really such a wizard? Well, the answer is yes and no. He was able to get the most out of his players and certainly taught them many life skills as well as basketball skills. I suppose that made him a "magician." However, his planning of practices and games and his attention to detail also made him a great mechanic. As he so eloquently stated: "Goals achieved with little effort are seldom appreciated and give no personal satisfaction." He was truly a great teacher as well as a coach. The point here is that most of us are a combination of being a mechanic and a magician. We just may lean more in one direction or another.

YOUR PERSONAL SKILLS

I'm sure you have some thoughts about your strengths and weaknesses as well as how you like to get your work accomplished. Are you the creative type that needs to work within the right moment and right environment to get things done or do you have more of the roll up your sleeves, bring on the work mentality? Neither is wrong and both can be productive. To get the most accurate answers to some of these questions, you might want to check with those who know you best.

SELF TEST

The following questions may enable you to see whether you fit more in the mechanic or the magician category. Try rating yourself with these questions and—without sharing your results with them—ask two other people to rate you as well. The two people can be a significant other, or someone who knows you very well in your personal life, and a co-worker, or someone who knows you well in your business life.

After receiving the results, compare notes and see how well you did in your self-assessment. This process will allow you to have great insight how others perceive you versus how you perceive yourself.

Once you've looked at the numbers on the different scales, sit down with the other two people that filled out your evaluation and discuss the results. It might give you some more in-depth information about who you are and how to get the most out of your talent.

WHO ARE YOU?

1. IF YOU HAD TO RATE YOURSELF AS A MECHANIC OR A MAGICIAN, WHAT NUMBER WOULD YOU GIVE YOURSELF? (1 – YOU ARE THE ULTIMATE MECHANIC; 10 – YOU ARE THE ULTIMATE MAGICIAN)

2. I AM MOST PRODUCTIVE WITH A SET SCHEDULE TO COMPLETE A TASK

3. WHEN EVALUATING A GOAL AND HOW TO GET THERE, I LIKE TO PLAN EACH STEP OF THE WAY AND HAVE ALL THE DETAILS TAKEN CARE OF

4. WHEN COMPLETING A TASK AT WORK, I FOLLOW AN EXACT PROCESS OR ORDER TO REACH THE END RESULT

5. I LIKE TO HAVE A LIST OF THINGS TO ACCOMPLISH VERSUS COMPLETING TASKS AS THEY COME UP

6. I HAVE A SPECIFIC TIME WHEN I ANSWER PHONE CALLS AND E-MAILS SO I DON'T GET DISTRACTED WITH MY OTHER PROJECTS

7. AT THE BEGINNING OF THE WEEK, I PLAN OUT MY MAIN TASKS TO BE ACCOMPLISHED

8. I PERFORM BEST IF I START AND FINISH ONE PROJECT AT A TIME

Were the other evaluations of yourself close to what you *thought* about yourself? If not, discuss the items with the other two people that evaluated you. Find out how they perceive you. There is no right or wrong with either category. It does, however, tell you a little bit about how you may perform at your best.

It is important to remember these questions don't only go to the magician or mechanic scale, but they can also, more simply, play a role in the type of personality you have and where you are efficient or changed in the efficiency department. It is very important to look at both the content and the context of the responses.

SUMMING UP

Remember, whether you're a mechanic or magician, hard work is a must! The way in which that hard work is approached is vastly different—not better or worse, just different. There have been great mechanics as well as magicians in sports and business, and of course, life in general.

Figure out which end of the spectrum you are closer to, then address your task accordingly. Be honest, be clear, plan your path.

Although we all want a clear vision as to where we are going and why, remember to think outside the box, promote creativity in yourself and others, listen to new ideas with an open mind, and welcome sessions that bring forth positive thoughts and positive change.

Having completed your self-evaluation, you can plot your course based on your findings. You might want to work on the areas that are in the middle of the spectrum rather than those at either end of the spectrum.

The primary goal with all of this is to know yourself, understand how you work best, and be aware of others. When you accept their differences you accept your own. Differences and diversity—those are what makes that little ball go from one side of the net to the other. That, and knowing yourself.

66 *We are what we repeatedly do.*
Excellence, therefore, is not an act,
but a habit. **"**
– ARISTOTLE

12.

Maximizing
Your Potential

This is your ultimate goal—if you chose it. Not a result, not an event, but the very reason of being. When I was a child dreaming of being a professional tennis player, I tried to figure out what my goal was. Where did I want to end up in the world rankings? How many tournaments did I want to win, etc.? It became very confusing and hard to do anything except dream.

In my mid-twenties, I decided the best goal I could have and the healthiest evaluation I could come up with was: I want to be 35 years old retired from playing professionally with no regrets—knowing I did everything possible to maximize my potential. That is where I left it and I felt enlightened by the process I went through to get there. The result-oriented marker can and will change as you make improvements or perhaps when you face stagnancy. At such times, patience and objectivity come into play. The goal is to find ways to enhance your game.

A great example of maximizing your potential can be seen in the career of Ivan Lendl. Ivan was a very good player on the tour for quite a while. Then he committed himself to becoming the fittest player on the tour. At that point, he became a great player.

Ivan started off as a promising junior player. He had early success when he became the No. 1-ranked junior in the world in 1978 and won the boys' singles titles at both the French Open and Wimbledon. Obviously, he was very talented. In the early 1980s Ivan won many matches and actually had a 44-match winning streak. However, even though he'd reached four Grand Slam tournament finals, a Grand Slam singles title had eluded him until he defeated McEnroe in the finals of the French Open in 1984, in a classic five-setter. This led to Ivan dominating tennis in the 1980s and winning a total of eight Grand Slam singles titles. Not bad for a guy that *Tennis Magazine* called "the game's greatest overachiever." To me, being called an overachiever is a great compliment. It truly highlights a player who absolutely got the most out of his game.

Another player who got the most out of his game is Brad Gilbert. Brad is obviously well-known as a tennis commentator on ESPN as well as the former coach of Agassi, Roddick and Murray. However, prior to his coaching and commentating, Brad was a player whom I viewed as a great strategist. After reaching the finals of the NCAA Championships in 1982, he played on the professional tennis tour for 14 years. Although Brad was not known for a huge serve, punishing ground strokes or exceptional volleys, he was a solid all-around player with a great mental approach to the game. His best skill, in my opinion, was to take his opponent out of his rhythm during a match. If Brad played a serve and volleyer, he would draw him into playing long baseline rallies. If he played a baseliner, Brad could be found attacking the net regularly. Playing this way, he was able to expose his opponents' weaknesses. He was also fiercely competitive and covered the court very well. With his unorthodox style of game—"winning ugly" as he called it—he reached No. 4 in the world in 1990 and won 20 titles on the pro tour. This included wins over some of the very best players at that time—Becker, Courier, Edberg, McEnroe, and Sampras. In addition, Brad won a bronze medal at the 1988 Seoul Olympics.

RECOGNIZING THE TRAITS OF SUCCESSFUL PEOPLE

Remember that just because personalities may be different, it does not mean that there aren't any similarities in the traits that lead to success. This can be very true when looking at elite athletes and other successful people. During my time with Pete, I had many people requesting me to teach their child to serve or hit a forehand like him. My response was (and still is): how about looking at the traits that enable your child to perform a specific skill and then see which ones we can incorporate to assist your child? Successful people are models in what they do, but it is generally healthier and probably more practical to emulate the traits and understand the process needed to execute them.

Both Ivan and Brad, each in their own way, reached their maximum potential. Clearly, there are some differences between these two players, starting with their career accomplishments. Ivan's eight Grand Slam singles titles and domination of tennis in the 80's sets him apart from others. In addition, Brad's background and upbringing in northern California were quite different from Ivan's Czech roots. Finally, their personalities could not be more different. Brad's gregarious nature and outgoing manner are the 180-degree opposite of Ivan's more reserved nature. However, if we look a little deeper underneath the surface, we find that these two players have a lot in common. When we bring Pete into the equation, we see some key traits they all share that helped each reach his full potential. Let's take a look at the similarities in their approaches and see how this might apply to your life.

DEDICATING YOURSELF TO YOUR TRUE POTENTIAL

Research has shown that the most important component in talent development is "drive" or "determination." From personal experience, I can clearly say that I have found the same in the players I have observed and/or worked with. This dedication is just as important in a business venture or in reaching any personal goal. If you don't have the passion to reach a certain "high watermark" and if you don't put in the effort to get there, you won't make it. Having dedication means focus, and being focused means having the ultimate goal right in front of you at all times.

PAYING YOUR DUES

This is closely related to the previous point. All three of the players mentioned—Brad, Ivan, and Pete—put in countless hours of practice and training when they were young to help reach their ultimate goal. There were no shortcuts. Although each player may have focused on different areas—Ivan's topspin backhand, Pete's one-handed backhand, and Brad's movement—they all wanted to find an edge and improve an already very strong game. If the proper desire is in place, then paying your dues is the admission price. After that, it's the journey… you will learn to enjoy this effort, because this is where you will spend most of your time. The ability to relentlessly pursue a goal while engaging in a process is a skill and a habit. But we must reinforce this habit. Great players and successful businessmen alike are able to deal with the bumps in the process. When it isn't going well, they accept the bump, and persevere, and thus they continue until it does go well.

BEING SELF-CONFIDENT

True self-confidence will only come into play when you know you have put in the proper effort. In tennis, this includes countless hours of training as well as learning how to play matches. Playing matches is important in seeing how you compare with others and to evaluate if you should move up a level or not. This is where it is important not to skip steps. Pete competed in tournaments as a junior and did relatively well, but didn't worry so much about winning these events because his focus was on success at the professional level. He had the self-confidence to see beyond the junior results and not to worry about winning each and every junior title. This did not mean he did not compete hard or that losing was any easier. It merely meant he had a grasp of his long term goals and vision and was not going to let things get in the way of his long term vision. Ivan's self-confidence grew when he improved his fitness to the point that he knew in his own mind that he wouldn't lose any

long matches. In fact, when he won that final in 1984, it was a positive verification of his hard work. To come back from two sets down to McEnroe and win a grueling five set match was the exact affirmation he needed to skyrocket his confidence to the next level.

True self confidence is not being self-involved, its being aware—*self-full* not *selfish,* as a wise psychologist once told me. The key to this is objectivity. You have to hold up that mirror and see yourself as you are. You need to take pride in your accomplishments. But, more important, you must own the process that leads to those accomplishments—when that is done in an objective manner, then true self-belief and confidence flow. They become fact, not boorish bravado. So, be clear and be honest. Take pride in delivering your presentation, or landing that acting role, or cleaning the kitchen. Whatever it is you do, seek excellence. In this way, the seeds you plant will grow, and surely blossom later on.

USING YOUR NATURAL TALENT

This is an area where all three players were a bit different from each other. Pete was clearly a very talented athlete. I am convinced that he could have been a very good baseball or basketball player as well— remember his jumping overhead? Brad played other sports as well and had the athlete's eye and skill to excel in other areas than tennis. Ivan played ice hockey as a youngster, but since his mother was an accomplished tennis player, he focused on tennis quite early. The main point is that it certainly doesn't hurt to be a "natural talent" but it's not as important as hard work in attaining success.

CONTINUING TO IMPROVE

Although every player hits plateaus, the goal is to continue to improve some component of your game. I had numerous discussions about this exact concept with Pete throughout his career. Early on when he did not want to come to the net as frequently, I stressed how necessary it was to continue to come forward, and to relentlessly work on it, so that he'd be more proficient in that area. As a result, by the end of the second week of Wimbledon, Pete was at his best at the net, and that was due to the effort he put in.

This theme should be consistent with all your endeavors. Just like the salesman who requires repetition to perform his message, or pitch, you should know that the more you do it, the better it will be. If you do not get it down the first time, keep doing it. Trust that it will evolve and progress. It may change shape and content, but if so, fine, you will be right with it, flowing with the change.

The salesman who "heard" his pitch learns from it when he is doubly aware of how well it's being received. Sales are his final reward, but during his journey, he is learning how receptive people are to his pitch. As he progresses, he gains confidence and efficiency.

The school teacher also has a kind of pitch. The clients are students. When the pitch is enthusiastic, no matter what the subject, the interest level of the client rises. The ancient Greeks used the motto *nihil sine labore* (nothing without work) but they were wise enough to know the quality of things. Quality teaching equals quality attention. What is quality? It's easier to define what it isn't. What it isn't is boring. When the salesman, the teacher, the performer are in the flow, all eyes are attentive. The pitch works.

And how, you might wonder, could this simple strategy apply to something like housekeeping? By being "present" and in the flow, the worker at any task becomes more efficient and does more work in less time. It's a matter of proficiency. Sampras' proficiency eventually reached levels of such grace that it didn't seem that he was competing, merely playing. And yet his results proved that he was competing at the very highest level.

The actor repeats his lines, gets them down, and in doing so learns that within the lines there is nuance, shading, and message beyond the mere words. There is emotive power in the way the lines are said. And so they slow down or speed up as the emotion subtly negotiates the curves and speedways of the drama.

Repetition enables fluidity and creates a kind of comfort zone wherein the player, performer, or worker is able to do his best work. On the tennis court, in the classroom, or the boardroom, it is all the same. As Zen master Shunryu Suzuki said, "to shine one corner of the world." This expresses both engagement, fully present kinetic connection and also repetition. The more you do it the better you like it, and the more you like it the more others like what you do! It, again, is all about what you see in the mirror. The happier the face you see the more likely the task will continue to be efficiently and effectively executed.

Some people, using this method of performing, shining, and growing—succeed over time so that they never stop developing. Brad is a great example of someone in the sport of tennis who continued to improve throughout his entire career. He made great strides from high school to junior college to college, and all the way to the pros. In fact, when Brad reached the pro level, the improvements in his game became more noticeable to me every step of the way. Lendl, once he'd won his first Grand Slam title, gained such singular confidence that his serve, volleys and his backhand improved constantly and almost immeasurably.

LOWERING THE VOLUME ON WEAKNESS

You may say that Pete looked the same no matter if he was winning or losing. This, in fact, was somewhat intimidating and disconcerting to his opponents. They never really knew what he was thinking or feeling. The enigmatic persona of Pete's was an advantage, and it left many players with nothing to gnaw on. Pete would shake hands, having won or lost, walk off the court, take care of his press responsibilities, and leave the tournaments with the same equable balance he came in with. His peers would not know what he was thinking or feeling and thus he gained an edge.

It is one thing to be open and honest, but it is another to talk too much. Regardless of your endeavor, it is necessary to find the perfect equilibrium between speaking, listening, and being. Sometimes no words are best. Absorb what has happened, evaluate, and don't jump to judgment. As they say, nothing is cast in bronze. But they also say nothing worthwhile should be taken for granted. An understanding of what you're doing and how you're doing it brings us back to the mirror. Shine it often, and you will see a different face in the reflection less and less. When the faces are identical in form and essence, you are probably playing your best and delivering your best message.

Of course, styles differ, as I have said earlier. The style of Ivan and Brad was not the Pete paradigm of silence. They tried to intimidate in a more outgoing manner. Ivan could (and would) punish players with his ground strokes. Players coming to the net knew they must be ready to possibly get hit. None of them wanted to give their opponent the upper hand even for a second. The forward effect of these two players was not like Pete's "what can you do to me?" and "you don't know what I can do to you."

Ivan and Brad were more outward, less mysterious, more in-your-face. While Pete's calm method implied that he might, just might, walk on water.

MAINTAINING FITNESS

Ivan's fitness routines were legendary and when he focused on it, he became nearly unbeatable for several years. He used this as an intimidation factor as well. I remember hearing about his grueling training sessions followed by 30-mile bike rides at breakneck speeds.

One time I had the pleasure of going to Ivan's house for a training block, and I was amazed by his discipline and work ethic. We practiced for two hours in the morning, then went back to his house for lunch, after which he excused himself for a nap for an hour and half. When he returned, we did another hour and half on the court, and then he was off on the bike.

The key thing here is consistency. Ivan's routine was habit and this habit just became second nature to him. Once your body encodes a training procedure that is well-wrought and disciplined, it will be like a dog waiting to go for a walk at a specific time—it will know even if you should forget. Most of us don't have time for a 30-mile bike ride, nor would we necessarily want to do that. But the point is to prioritize your exercise schedule, and make it work for you while you work for it.

I have a close friend, a businessman who has a 5 a.m. ritual of getting up to use the StairMaster. He says this has really helped him stay in shape and it's also kept his mind sharp during the day. Of course, there's no one-size-fits-all type of exercise routine to follow. Consult your local trainer and physician for the appropriate advice. Then seek a physical challenge that makes you feel good. This will pay dividends in your professional and personal life as well.

Improving your fitness will not only benefit you in a sport of your choice, but it can help sharpen your workday skills as well. When the body is invigorated and fit, the mind is too. Endorphins encourage optimism; so does habitual practice. The ancient Greeks, among the world's supreme athletes, believed in the linkage of body, mind, and spirit. Repetitive workouts bring all of these to the fore.

Current studies show that fitness helps us in more ways than one. We seem to know this, but we don't always practice it.

The beauty of physical activity is that it can quickly benefit you mentally and physically. It does so many things at once. It raises energy levels, helps to achieve greater discipline, assists in your ability to focus on the task at hand. These are all key components to achieving any goal.

For the numbers cruncher who is bent behind a desk, for the researcher who is bound to the computer screen, for the coach who sits on a bench watching a ball move back and forth across a court, physical activity is a blessing. The yoga workshop, the spin class at the gym, or just walking the dog, all are simple activities that can rest your mind and sharpen the edge of your thinking. Physical activity is the fastest and most beneficial "drug" known to humankind.

HOLDING UP THE MIRROR

Looking at yourself in athletics suggests you can also learn by watching others. For example, there are similarities between Brad and Ivan that are worthy of being noticed. Take a look below.

1. BOTH WERE COMPLETELY DEDICATED

2. EACH WAS RESILIENT AND PAID DUES AS A HARD WORKER

3. EACH GAINED SELF-CONFIDENCE AS HIS CAREER PROGRESSED

4. BOTH MEN WERE UNDERESTIMATED, YET IN SPITE OF THIS
REACHED A HIGH LEVEL OF SUCCESS

5. NEITHER ONE WAS KNOWN AS A "GREAT NATURAL TALENT"

6. EACH CONTINUED TO IMPROVE THROUGHOUT HIS CAREER

7. NEITHER MAN REVEALED WEAKNESSES TO AN OPPONENT

8. BOTH MADE FITNESS A LARGE PART OF HIS IMPROVEMENT POTENTIAL

By holding up the mirror, as I've been saying, these players gained a new perspective on who they were, how they played, and why they were in the game. Try this out yourself. When you look at yourself, literally, in the mirror, what do you see? What kind of player, person, worker? When you hold your work up to the mirror, what do you see? What kind of excellence is there to examine? Does it fall short of your goal? Does it meet it head-on? How far away is your goal from your reach? Remember, in your own evaluation, treat yourself with objectivity. Be honest but not debilitating. And always remember, it isn't the destination but the journey that shapes it that is so important. If you are enjoying getting there, you're going to like being there.

66 *By persisting in your path, though you forfeit the little, you gain the great.* **99**
– RALPH WALDO EMERSON

13.

What is the
Big Picture?

Sampras and Federer are uniquely skilled in understanding the Big Picture and how best to trust their skills in the most pressure-filled moments.

t's easy to get caught up in what we see right in front of us and to forget the big picture that encompasses what's behind and in front of us. What happens is that our immediate environment takes precedence over everything: short range results give us a temporary feeling of success or failure. This is, no doubt, a slippery slope. How can we process what's happening as it's happening? We can't, which is why interviews with boxers at the end of a match often conclude with: "I will have to see the tape."

We require feedback to evaluate and move forward, but this also means we can't get wrapped up in the emotion of the moment, as it could easily deter us from the big picture. Hence the boxer after a big loss saying, "I will have to get together with my manager and see where things go next." And how about the fighter who has just managed to pull off a very big win? If he's smart, he won't allow himself to be so satisfied that he forgets his mission, his goal, and the road ahead.

In everyday situations many of us tend to lose our focus in just this way. Either we feel negatively about our performance or we feel euphorically convinced that it's going to be even easier next time. Either way we lose—both mentally and spiritually.

The big picture includes the end view of a process-led journey. It follows a prioritized list of desired goals. And it allows us the best possible chance of realizing them.

No matter what the endeavor, you've got to be clear about what you're doing, how it's being done, and where it's taking you. The prioritized way you see this paradigm for success keeps you positively focused on the correct path. There is no hit or miss about this and there is in fact a kind of science to it, that is, a methodology that involves rational objectivity rather than random emotion.

I remember that some years ago, 17-year-old Justin Gimelstob was curled up in a ball of disappointment after losing a very tough tennis match at the Easter Bowl, a national junior tennis tournament.

Justin was beside himself because he'd blown a huge lead only to succumb to self-imposed pressure and expectation. I felt terrible that he had to go through this, yet, I had a very good understanding of what had happened. I wondered, if this match, in the grand scheme of things, mattered as much as he thought it did. Was this going to be a defining moment in his tennis career?

Here was this very talented American junior tennis player who hoped to be a professional, but who was overly undone because of one tennis match at the junior level.

I thought maybe there was a way that I could let him have his disappointment, but also show him that it was merely piece number 13 in the big picture, 5,000 piece jigsaw puzzle.

From a coaching perspective, this concept was not hard to see. However, getting it across to Justin or any youngster, right then, was going to be a tough task. At 17, Justin was an emotionally volatile adolescent whose investment in the event of the moment was huge.

At any age and any stage, you might be well-advised to imagine the big-picture puzzle scenario. By objective reflection, you can see all the pieces of the puzzle even though some of them are blurred and others are mysterious. Still they're all there and they each have a specific purpose. The goal is to get better and better at handling the ebb and flow of life's challenges. It helps to know that missing parts can come together, and that you have the skill and the intelligence to see how they fit together with that larger picture.

Practically speaking, there are things we can do to evaluate our intended success or supposed failure at any given moment. The first step is to know, deep down, that it's a journey, not a game of bingo or a trophy contest. It's neither gambling nor mysticism.

Once you firmly believe in the journey, categorize and prioritize the desired short-term results based on the set up of your short term process. Where does the one event, the Gimelstob scenario, so to put it, fit into your own big picture? Where does it fit into your long-term end game?

It's important to give yourself some perspective, and balance and then move on. I'm not naive; I realize the passion and emotion that goes into so many of life's endeavors can be challenging to manage, but this too is a learning process. You should feel what you are feeling, then absorb, evaluate and objectively move forward. As the great frontiersman Davy Crockett once said, "Be sure you're right, then go ahead."

One time when my daughter was really disappointed that she'd gotten an 88 on an exam, and this dismal failure had rocked her world, I asked her if it really mattered if she got an 88 versus a 92. I asked, "How is this going to impact your life? How will this one score affect what you're going to do or who you're going to be later in life?"

Most importantly, I asked her if she was satisfied with how she'd prepared for the exam. When she said yes, I told her that this was, in fact, more important than the score. I said, "If the preparation was good and you were ready for the exam, then, next time, your study habits will create the right environment for you to achieve more positive results."

Sure, it would be great to get perfect scores and perfect results whenever you wanted to, but that isn't possible, nor even preferable. With such odds, why play?

All that is possible is to evaluate your process and see if you gave yourself the best chance to achieve the best result. In this way, you can see where your small puzzle piece fits into the big picture.

In the end, the big picture is about process. It is about your skills and abilities of course. But it's also about the step-by-step shaping of your long range goals.

The ability to set up the surroundings is what drives the process to the triumphant result.

It's too easy to get tangled up in *I have to win*. Better to see what to *do* in order to be a winner. And that, again, is being able to visualize process.

When I talked to Roger about the strategy of the day, it was not based on the result. Instead it was about the best way he could be most effective given the environment he was in on that day.

So, if you can execute A, B, and C, you will be very effective and create an opportunity where you give yourself the best chance for your talents to shine. One day's shining is all about the big picture. What do I want to achieve? How does today fit into that larger scenario? And most important, where will it point me?

CHECK YOURSELF

It's very easy to get caught up in the emotion of the moment. When we do this, we lose sight of the big picture. Remember the short-term goals you've set (results and process) point to where you want to be at the end. If you do not achieve the result-oriented short-term goals, it doesn't mean you won't reach your desired target at the journey's finish.

What it does mean is this: You need to make sure you are following your process correctly while pursuing the short-term goals.

HOW DO YOU DO THAT?

1. TAKE A DEEP BREATH AND LOOK AT THE PROCESS FIRST.
DID THE PROCESS LET YOU DOWN, OR WAS IT THE EXECUTION OF IT?

2. UNDERSTAND THE MANNER IN WHICH YOU HANDLED THE PROCESS…
IF IT'S NOT UP TO YOUR EXPECTATION YOU COULD BE ENCOUNTERING LETDOWN,
AND THEREBY DETRACTING FROM A HIGHER LEVEL OF EXECUTION.

3. ADJUST AND MAKE CORRECTIONS SO THESE EXECUTION ISSUES
DO NOT REPEAT THEMSELVES.

4. UNDERSTAND THAT THIS SHORT-TERM RESULT IS PART OF THE OVERALL JOURNEY,
NOT AN END IN ITSELF, NOT A FINAL DESTINATION.

A proud but bittersweet moment:
beating friend and tennis legend
John McEnroe at the U.S. Open.

Each time you don't reach your goal, consider this: Now you have another opportunity to learn, so that you can reach the plateau in your next round of activity.

Objectivity is the key component to learning. As they say, live and learn, no matter where you are or what you are doing. This enables you to stay on the path. It also reinforces the big picture so that you forfeit the little to gain the great.

66 *One of the signs of nervousness is*
the abandoning of your game plan. **"**
– MALIVAI WASHINGTON

14.

How to Banish
a Negative Sense
of Inevitability

W hat, you might ask, allows us to fall into the opposite path of the champion's way? What gets you off your game and promotes a negative sense of inevitability?

Bad habits, fear, insecurity, lack of discipline, lack of focus? Probably all of the above.

It is in our nature to have fear or doubt and that can get compounded when we are trying to achieve excellence. Whether it be an athletic endeavor, an administrative role, or merely a job around the house, the thought and the consequence of failure can enter into it and appear more severe depending on the situation. As the philosopher once said, it is all a matter of degree, but once again, the panacea is process, and with a plan firmly in place, you can see the positive result at the finish line—even when you're not there yet.

In my experience, the initial process of trying to accomplish a task is generally smooth. Yet as we move forward, the perceived consequences of our actions creep in, and with them negativity.

Once the what-ifs take over, we are already being drawn away from our process and thus our focus is diminished. Once that starts it is very easy to get into a situation where the process is clouded with an internal dialogue that quickly turns to negativity and doubt. This is not always easy to spot at the outset. You can't see it and therefore you can't tell yourself, "Here I go again."

Again, this is a common occurrence and part of human nature. With good habits, disciplined preparation, and execution, you can conquer these uneasy feelings and downward-pulling tendencies and turn them into the positive sense of inevitability. Positive reinforcement in a process-oriented environment, structured by task execution and clarity will be the right building blocks for success. Once you see the big picture and your manner of getting out of the smaller one, things will improve readily. Steadfast resiliency is also a tool that will get you through any adversity, including doubt, insecurity and lack of belief. There is a lot to be said for the old cliché, "Fake it till you make it."

In his book *The Power of Right Thinking,* Dr. Frank Crane says, "The greatest source of power in the world is the thought of a human brain. Your net efficiency can be measured by the forces of what you think. Thoughts are more durable than things."

Naturally, some types of adversity and setbacks are out of our control. At times, the best advice I can offer is that we need to accept the curve of the road—or sometimes, suddenly, no visible road at all. With acceptance comes understanding and then we can recover and move on. Such things happen occasionally in the flash of an eye, so we must be ready at all times for the unexpected.

This is where both perspective and understanding become so important. What are the common pitfalls? The ones we are likely to encounter at every stage of the game of life?

PUTTING THE CART BEFORE THE HORSE

This is a common occurrence and happens at all levels of development. In the midst of a task, competition, or any endeavor, our mind may wander. In doing so, we often speed things up to the end of whatever we are doing. Once there, we start to think about what is in store for us—*The Lady, or The Tiger,* as the famous story is titled. On the one hand, we have achievement and on the other, perceived failure. The mind plays in the field of dreams, but dreams can also turn to nightmares quite quickly.

The negative thoughts say to us, "Uh oh, here we go again." This is a self-fulfilling prophecy and it is the epitome of the negative sense of inevitability. The mind leads us astray from the process of what is next, and takes the positive viewpoint away, so that we move forward in fear, doubt, and denial. Worst of all, we lose the ability to focus on the process. And it is the process that is our assurance, our mainstay. It is our way of staying in the present moment.

So, let's rewind and get back into the process again. Let's return to the step-by-step consciousness that connects us to the NOW. Focus on the present, but be ready to focus on the next step, which will soon be right there in front of your face.

I remember early on when I was coaching Pete and I asked him about the draw. and how far ahead he looked at the start of the tournament.

Pete said, "Well, I just focus on one match at a time. Sometimes through the media, I hear who is in my area of the draw, but what's the point of thinking about who I might play in the quarterfinals when I have to win four matches to even get to the quarters of a Grand Slam. It's wasted energy and focus to lose yourself in anything that might happen."

Wasted energy occurs when we allow ourselves—right in the middle of something—to jump ahead in our mind's eye and take a little spin into the future. Right there, in that moment, we get off-point and out of focus. And the process devolves without us even knowing it.

Pete was superb at staying bright and alert and always in the present, and this was a key ingredient in his recipe for success.

DEALING WITH PERCEIVED FAILURES

During our journey we will ultimately have many failures and successes. The "wins" will warrant happiness and celebration while the failures will tend to send us down a path of depression and unfulfilled promise.

This does not have to be the case. We can use the loss or the perceived failure as a catalyst to move forward.

We can easily go back and evaluate where and why we got off track. The ability to see clearly what happened, mentally and physically, will allow us to move forward in a positive way. It will also help us to avoid a negative sense of inevitability in the future.

We can learn from what went wrong in the past—as long as we don't overindulge in this—but best of all we can hold on to the way forward and not make the same mistakes again. "When you see the turn, lean into it," said the runner, who remembered stumbling. But now, in remembering, he only sees himself leaning in against the wind and keeping on even harder than before so that the old memory is welded positively into the new.

Early in my career I had a terrific opportunity. I was playing Mats Wilander at the U.S. Open and had two sets points to go ahead two-sets-to-one in a best-of-five-sets match. I played one poor point and Mats played one terrific point to get even. He then won the set and I fell apart. I was so very close and yet I lost my concentration for five minutes and then I was down two-sets-to-one and 4-1 in the fourth set. The match was over.

I came off the court and said I was never going to let my mind wander like that again. I was going to deal with adversity and failure differently. I was going to train my mind to stay where it should be—in the now—not in the netherworld of the future.

Two weeks later I was playing Stefan Edberg in the final of a tournament in Los Angeles and we had a topsy-turvy match where I got the lead and he came back, then he took the lead and I could either dig in or "go away" mentally. I was so proud that I was able to play each point and deal with the ebb and flow of the match without losing my concentration.

As a result, I won the match in a tie-breaker in the third set. This was my first professional tournament victory. One of my proudest moments.

It wasn't necessarily because the win was against such a terrific player, but because of my own personal commitment to rebound from a very difficult loss where my mind had led me astray. This time I'd stayed the course, seeing each thing as it came, one shot at a time, with steely-eyed, maximum focus. That was what got me the win.

We can turn our failures into the magical tools we use to create our triumphs. It is not a matter of hit or miss. It's a matter of being there, fully, with an empty, positive, clear-sighted eye. Our entire life—professional and personal—is a journey, not a destination, as I keep saying in this book. I suppose we cannot say it enough. We must remind ourselves so that the journey is itself the joy of being there.

DEALING WITH HIGHS AND LOWS—WHY CAN'T I DO WHAT I SEE IN MY MIND?

This is a common question and it occurs to every one of us at one time or another. The main challenge in dealing with highs and lows is to keep a steady mind and an even emotional barometer.

Walking on to Centre Court at Wimbledon, I remembered a line from Rudyard Kipling's poem: *See if you can meet with Triumph and Disaster and treat those two impostors just the same.*

Of course it's not easy. If we constantly feel like we're on an emotional roller coaster after each victory or failure, then we are setting ourselves up for a mental beating. The "two imposters" in that case are always the winners.

The highs and lows on tour (as in life) are a great challenge for anyone, but much of the progress I have witnessed in players is about maturity and experience.

I remember in 2014 when Sloane Stephens lost a quarterfinal match in Birmingham, England, just prior to Wimbledon. She had not played well on that day and was evidently distraught. Leading in I felt that Sloane had been hitting the ball well but she just was just brutal on herself very quickly that day. This was caused by her reactions to poor shots early in the match. So, in that moment, her mind became clouded and she was unable to think clearly, and try to win with her "average" level.

No question, this was a tough day and it bothered Sloane for some days after as well. Leading into the next tournament in Eastbourne, she did rebound and started to play better, but it took a bit longer to get to that stage. Much of this uneven timeline happened because Sloane was still at an earlier stage in her career and hadn't been through the tour scenario often enough.

Now, years later, Sloane's progress is different. I am seeing her rebound more quickly and even winning tournaments after an average result. This is a testimony to her evolution as an athlete. She is clearly becoming more efficient and effective in overcoming adversity. This is great to see in anyone but especially in tennis players, where everyone loses every week except one person…not the best of odds, I would say.

Success should feel great and failure should hurt, but neither one should dictate to us who we are or what we can be when we try even harder and smarter. That's when we dethrone the imposters, overthrow the win-lose complex, and become who we really are, players in the game of life.

In 2011 Roger Federer lost a two-sets-to-love lead to Jo-Wilfried Tsonga in the quarterfinals of Wimbledon and lost a heartbreaking match. That was the first time in his career he had lost from a two-sets-to-love lead.

Once Roger's media commitments were done we headed back to his house and he dropped his bags and within five minutes he was on his hands and knees laughing and playing with his young daughters in the backyard. It was terrific to see this, and to know it was honestly the way he felt at that moment. Letting go is easier when you actually do it often enough so that it becomes second nature.

We were talking later in the evening about the ability, and the willingness to move on.

Roger said, "Look, losing hurts, but what's done is done. We've talked about it, I understand what happened, now let's learn and move on. I am not going to let something in one part of my life mess up my whole life."

Sounds pretty simple, right?

So difficult though when you are invested in what you're trying to do. It takes a certain kind of character and perspective to manage this well. I would also have to say it takes practice, patience, and self-belief.

YOU HAVE TO KEEP THE PICTURE
OF POSITIVITY IN YOUR MIND.

YOU NEED TO KEEP THE PROCESS CLEAR,
SHARP, AND FRESH BY RE-EXAMINING IT.

YOU MUST REMAIN COMMITTED AND MAKE
SURE TO UTILIZE ALL OF YOUR RESOURCES.

In reasoning things out, it's often necessary to go over the past—but not to dwell on it. Once you understand it, you can see that it won't always happen that way. For good or ill, the imposters may flicker into your mind again. But in the same way Roger let them go, and played spontaneously with his children, you can play in your own field of dreams. With a joyful belief in yourself the negative sense of inevitability is firmly replaced by the positive sense of inevitability. It is a matter of choice, habit, plan, and focus. A smile doesn't hurt either.

In 2015, Sloane Stephens learned to win more playing "average" tennis, a skill that, down the road, leads very good players to greatness.

66 *A pessimist sees the difficulty in every opportunity; an optimist sees the opportunity in every difficulty.* **"**
– WINSTON CHURCHILL

15.

How to Keep a Positive Sense of Inevitability

Not long ago I observed Roger Federer explain training, preparation, and professional behavior to a 20-year-old during one of our training sessions. This reminded me of my younger days as a professional athlete. Seeing a 30-year-old champion like Roger drenched in sweat at the side of a sun-baked court talking to a young professional, who even though exhausted was focused on every syllable Roger uttered...again, it brought me back to my own beginnings.

I remember having a similar conversation with Ivan Lendl at his house when I was a young professional. I was searching, trying to be the best I could be, but perhaps I was looking for something that wasn't quite there, or more importantly, maybe something that was right there—right in front of my face!

Now, as I watched Roger and listened to him speak, I knew that young Ricardas Berankis was soaking it up, for this was quintessential Roger Federer. The aesthetic of his mastery was coming across loud and clear even when he spoke softly.

"Work hard," he said, "Be consistent in your approach, enjoy your life and be patient. Don't rush, plan well, take care of your body and your mind." Roger's message was elemental. But how was it being received? And how might it be implemented in Ricardas' future career? That, of course, remains to be seen.

The young Paul Annacone heard similar things from Ivan. How would it work for him? Well, I smile when I think back on that. Perhaps young Paul went too far, too fast. Maybe he missed the "be patient" part.

I believe, all things considered, I lost perspective. I didn't quite grasp the emotional calm I might've gained from the big picture mentality that was paramount in making it all work. Was I building the path to a positive sense of inevitability? Probably not.

It's common with young people to imagine "this is it." The pressure begins there, and because they are less emotionally mature, and perhaps more volatile and less stable, the balance is tipped in favor of more passion but less patience. For that positive sense of inevitability we are looking for, the athlete, the student, or the businessman or woman needs to take a deep breath and open the eyes wider to encompass the whole and not just a part of the picture.

When you are younger and less experienced, you need to have good habits so deeply ingrained that the positive sense of inevitability is secure in your heart and mind. More importantly, you have to expand your emotional field of vision to successfully deal with the unpredictable nature of reality. The results may not be there immediately. But don't be discouraged. The mind will lead the body and positive results will come as you improve the execution of each new move.

When you submit to a loss of perspective, you generally tend to lose focus on the task at hand. Thus, the conversation between player and play diminishes. In all likelihood, this will negatively affect your performance.

To avoid early burn-out, you will need to do two things: Stay in tune with your process and stay in the moment. Remain on the page where performance is the logical outcome of the detailed process set up for success.

Often, then, it's necessary to take a step back, clear your mind about "potential perceived consequences" and get back to reality. This means concentrating on what is next.

So, what is the next step in the process? Did we skip one and two in our race to get to three?

All right… so we messed up three as a result of forgetting one and two… what to do?

Well, don't beat yourself up about it. Check the plan book and then dive into the execution again.

I am looking at Roger now, with his legs crossed on the bench towel draped over his head after completing a grueling drill. He's relaxed, composed, ready for the next task.

Across the court I see young Ricardas a little down, a lot tired, trying to find another gear.

Patience Ricardas, it will come.

When we lose focus, the mind starts to wonder about the viability of achieving the result we've planned on. We start asking, *Can I do this? Am I on track? What will happen if…?*

The *what if* mentality adds the potential for negativity to creep into the picture.

Cut to: Roger, relaxed with a bottle of water in hand, knowing the work's been done for the day, time to move on to… life.

This didn't just happen for Roger or for Pete or any other great pro you care to name. It was learned, it was practiced. And it is all on the map of how to get the positive sense of inevitability.

Desire, which is a good thing, can turn into unwarranted hunger that can often lead to panic and insecurity. Be clear, be committed, and be patient. Let tempered passion lead you along the process-oriented path that gets you to a place where you can go through each step again and again until you are assured that things will work out the way you want them to.

Pete didn't roll out of bed and hit 130-mph serves on the line in pressure-packed scenarios, one after another. He practiced it, he lived it, and he hit thousands upon thousands of serves.

What you don't think about when you imagine a man like Pete is that sometimes he missed. Sometimes he failed. But the more he hit them, the more they went in and the more they went in, the more that positive sense of inevitability grew and ultimately blossomed into the baseline theme that a champion maintains throughout his career.

There are many young tennis players with too much emotion given to each and every shot. I remember standing behind Justin Gimelstob during a practice session at UCLA some years ago. He was continually throwing out comments, negatively judging many of his shots. I stood by silently watching and after about 10 minutes he turned to me and said, "Paul, what do you think?"

I replied, "Justin, sometimes you just miss…just keep hitting."

I'm not sure he was thrilled with my response, but the point is, sometimes things just don't go in, sometimes they go out—welcome to life as it is lived in the real world. Get back to your plan, get ready for the next serve—yours or theirs—be ready to execute with a positive attitude.

.   .   .   .

From 2007–10 I worked as the head coach of men's tennis for The Lawn Tennis Association in England. This was the most challenging environment I had been in as far as trying to instill this primal lesson of positive attitude, and positive sense of inevitability.

There were many years where the development of players in England had been below par or at least below expectation. Although Tim Henman had done extremely well, there were not enough "layers" of players at all the different levels to support the growth of the sport and ultimately to promote the game at the professional level. This is extremely complex because Wimbledon is right there in London, and with that proximity comes expectation of home-grown champions, and that wasn't what was happening.

What was happening was this: an environment of resentment was growing through the media and the tennis community. This resentment exacerbated the relatively shallow talent pool that was there. As a result of such negativity, the players felt it too. Fear of failure—the precise antithesis of the positive sense of inevitability—became a typical dominant, if unvoiced, point of view. Expectation and passion were still high, but so was the perception of failure.

"Uh-oh, what's gonna happen if I lose?" This question all by itself can lose a match. And when this is a fundamental theme, it's very tough to get back on the road of optimism and back on the road to process.

You can readily see why it's so important to start the education early on. Build that road of positivity when the child is young, then when adversity comes later on—as it almost surely will sometime or other—the default response will be an optimistic one.

This choice is really up to you. You can practice by reinforcing yourself positively or negatively. The real question is: Do you know when you're being positive? Do you know when you're being negative? Each day we should wake up and be aware of the inner dialogue that spells challenge, not the one that underscores defeat. We must also realize that no choice is actually making a choice. Emotions, the unconscious will, the bad habits that have accumulated within us are like silent judges. The way out, the exit ramp, so to say—is this: Be aware, be mindful. Insert the key that engages that positive sense of inevitability. Do you hear the engine running?

. . . .

In my experience from being around Pete, Roger, and many others, there is a certain pattern to the champion's way. No matter what level they are playing at, they will find a way to win, a way to move on, a way to get the result they want. The big question is how can we, the rest of us, learn how to translate the will and the way to win into what we do every day. This is our greatest challenge in life, not just in sports.

In the spring of 1995, Pete was not having a great clay court season, and had lost relatively early in all of his clay court tournaments. We were now headed to grass courts of England to play an event at Queen's Club ahead of Wimbledon.

During our travels together, I asked Pete on his thoughts about the clay court and how he was feeling about going to England.

A quiet calm came into his voice when he said, "I think there were a couple tough matches during the clay, maybe I was thinking too much and analyzing a bit too much. But I prepared well and worked hard, so it'll pay off."

I asked, "Anything in particular you think we need to focus on leading into Wimbledon?"

Pete answered, "No, just have to get the right-serve-and-return mentality and get in the grass court frame of mind, it'll be fine."

I remember being taken aback by how self-assured and cool-headed he was about this. I mean, he was just 23 years old at the time.

That calm—the Sampras trademark—paid big dividends. Pete went on to win both the Queen's Club tournament and Wimbledon that year. After the tournament, when we had a little down time, I asked him about the process… that spring hadn't gone great, what were his feelings?

Pete said, "Look, it's pretty simple. When I play well I will win. I'm fortunate to have enough talent so that when things are good, I generally will win. So, that's easy. But what happens when things don't go great? That's where I have to just focus and realize, that if I am there mentally and keep playing each point, I will probably win even if I am not playing great. I just feel like I'll find a way—even if my level isn't where I want it."

It seemed so simple. The powerful, unreserved and resilient inner belief that no matter what's there on the day, "I will find a way."

The way Pete said this so clearly reminded me that the positive sense of inevitability is a choice, a practiced trait. It doesn't just happen. It isn't a stroke of luck, as people like to say. It's practiced, and it is learned.

Make this your default mode. Constantly remind yourself of the positive possibilities based on the hard work you have put in. Make yourself see that there is a way, even when the way cannot be seen or imagined. It is there. Find it.

In the autumn of 2011, Roger lost a very tough five-set match in the semifinals of the U.S. Open after holding two match points. I remember going back to the hotel with him afterwards and watching him joyfully playing with his twin girls on the floor. I was in awe of his transition. He was freely expressing himself as if he'd never been in that emotional dungeon of the loss.

Interview with Sloane after she captured her first WTA title in Washington, D.C., during the summer of 2015.

That night we spoke about the loss but we ended up discussing the rest of the fall season. It was clear in Roger's untroubled voice that the remainder of the year was a great opportunity.

We were both sure about how to proceed, and what the process would be, but it was up to him to execute.

Two-and-a-half months later, Roger finished the season winning 17-straight singles matches, including two Davis Cup matches, and three tournaments in succession.

Truly, a champion's positive sense of inevitability.

So, how do you create this positive sense of inevitability?

1. HABITS! REINFORCE YOURSELF IN A POSITIVE WAY!

2. TRUST YOUR PROCESS

3. MAINTAIN PERSPECTIVE

4. WORK HARD TO PREPARE FOR ADVERSITY

5. EMBRACE ADVERSITY, DON'T FEAR IT

6. EMBRACE THE FACT THAT YOU ARE ONLY AS GOOD AS YOUR AVERAGE DAY'S PERFORMANCE

If you have confidence that this will lead to a positive sense of inevitability, you are on the path to the champion's way.

66 *Don't neglect the little things.* **99**
– DR. FRANK CRANE

16.
My Daily Planner

H ow many of us spend time floating through our day without a plan? A good many of us, I would suppose.

I have found that a prioritized list of things we want to accomplish is a great way to get on track and build good habits. I am a daily planner person, and I keep regular notes on how my day is going.

Here are a few key topics to consider for your own planning process:

1. TIME MANAGEMENT

2. FOCUS ON PRIORITIES

3. ATTENTION TO DETAIL

4. REST AND RECOVERY

TIME MANAGEMENT

Most of us have said, at one time or another: "What I need is more hours in the day!"

In truth, however, we don't need more hours. We need our daily planner. By efficient planning, we can create the sense of "more time" since we are spending our time more effectively.

This is to say that as you go through your tasks you can prioritize them so you know your level of urgency for each category. This too is very important. If you spend too much time on your menial tasks, the ones that need more attention to detail will inevitably get passed over. So, as you make your list, prioritize the things you need to do with a star or a number so you know where to focus your energy the most during the hours that have been allotted for this.

As Team Federer went through our training blocks we knew where the priorities were and how to make best use of the time depending on where we were in the training process.

You too can do this, personally and professionally, but efficiency is a key component to managing your time well. You want to make sure the priorities on your list are emphasized according to time slots in the overall process. For instance, in our training blocks with Roger, initially it's the physical aspect of the training that's focused on, while the tennis component gets built in and emphasized further along. We know this is most effective. If Roger is not fit and strong and does not have that good physical base, it's silly to push him hard on the practice court because this will cause frustration, and more importantly, may lead to injury.

So, build your base first, then branch out from there.

FOCUS ON PRIORITIES

It is just as important to understand what your priorities are as it is to work hard. If you spend too much time on the wrong thing it is going to badly influence your game plan.

This does not mean you should neglect areas you are not strong in; or eliminate tasks that are not as important. It means prioritize, get to things in due course, make a list and check tasks off but do so in a manner that deals with an emphasis that will get you the end result you want. You want positive gain, not stasis.

A terrific example of this occurred during my own tennis development. As I was moving up the rankings I had many people saying that I really needed to work on my ground strokes to become a better and more well-rounded player. So, I spent a lot of long hard hours doing exactly this.

The consequence was that I neglected my strengths, stopped spending the right amount of time on the things I was already doing well, and as a result my game suffered. I was disciplined and I worked hard, but I did not work *smart*. Your daily planner has to be smart and should relate specifically to your needs. Keep working on your strengths and make sure the areas that need the time, get the time they need too! This can only be done with a list of priorities.

During my time with Sloane, I tried to focus on her strengths. Sloane has a huge forehand and is a terrific athlete; so we set up our training program to work on patterns for success that were focused primarily on these two elemental areas. When you are aware of what you do best, you can set up success by doing what you do best *as often as possible*.

ATTENTION TO DETAIL

This is an area we can all improve on. When I would speak with Roger about his tennis and we were working together, I was more concerned about the level of intensity and specificity versus the amount of hours he might utilize to do it. So, we would look at one area and really focus on the details of getting it better. In other words, we set out to reach a certain realistic comfort level in executing a strategy or technique.

Generalities are fine and can help get you in a mindset to do something, but you need to narrow down the range of your activities. It comes down to specifics: you must be clear on what you are trying to accomplish. Get this message clear in your mind so you know not only what you are going to do, but how you are going to do it. Then, having put in the appropriate amount of time, check it off on your priority list!

REST AND RECOVERY

Most people don't realize the importance of rest and recovery. It's old school to merely think "no pain, no gain" or "work 'til you drop." Working smart is much different than just working hard. By working smart you give yourself time to rest and recover.

Your daily planner has to include rest and recovery. By virtue of making your itemized lists and by taking the time to sit down and construct this with care, you should be more able to plan your rest and recovery along with everything else.

When I went through the checklist with Team Federer after a long day's work, I knew Roger would shut down mentally and physically, because he knew the work had already been done. He wouldn't spend emotional energy wondering, "Did I do all the work?" or "Did I miss something?" We spent plenty of time setting up the process so when the plan was completed at the end of the day, we had dotted the "i's" and crossed the "t's."

It's only with a refreshed mind and body that you can truly move on to the next day, and the next task and feel cheerful about it. Give yourself the luxury of making rest and recovery part of your plan.

As I have said, during training blocks with Roger Federer, our team got together and put forth a collective plan for the period ahead. Whether it be two weeks, three weeks or 10 days, we had a blueprint of what the time will look like.

Whether you are an athlete, a student, a homemaker, plumber or decorator, you can do the same. This will help you prioritize your "to do" list and give you a plan that will increase your focus, and thus, your performance. Attention to detail is critical but it must not be slavish or foolish; it must be realistic.

Your plan should hit on all the prioritized areas of your life. You will have professional "to do's" and personal "to do's." You can mark each down in the manner of its urgency, and as you go along, you can evaluate your level of effectiveness.

I have found that task-oriented staging gives me a clear picture of what I need to do on a given day, week or month. It all ties together and becomes my indispensable, daily planner.

AS A TENNIS PLAYER YOU TAKE CARE OF ALL YOUR CATEGORIES:

1. TECHNICAL WORK ON YOUR SHOTS

2. MATCH SITUATIONS FOR STRATEGY

3. STRENGTH AND CONDITIONING

4. DIET AND NUTRITION

5. PSYCHOLOGICAL AND EMOTIONAL WELL-BEING

6. REST AND RECOVERY

7. PROFESSIONAL/SPONSOR RELATED ACTIVITY

As you go through each of the above categories you make your prioritized lists and then get them accomplished in a timely way that emphasizes the priorities.

As this process unfolds, you should make notes of how well you did and, further, what to do next to improve.

The key thing here is setting up a consistent process of good habits that give you a map of achievement for both short- and long-term goals.

As things move along you then have documentation of how it went—this way you can improve and adjust to be even more effective as you move forward.

HERE ARE SOME MORE IMPORTANT THINGS TO REMEMBER.

1. THE PLANNER HELPS GIVE YOU THE LIST TO ACHIEVE AN END RESULT

2. MAKE SURE THE TASKS RELATE TO THE END GAME YOU WANT—WHETHER IT IS A RESULT OR JUST THE ACCUMULATION OF DIVERSIFIED TASKS TO REACH THE OVERALL GOAL

3. EVALUATE YOUR LIST OR THE EFFECTIVENESS OF IT

4. EVALUATE HOW WELL THE TASKS ON THE LIST LEAD YOU TO THE END RESULT YOU ARE AIMING FOR

5. AND, FINALLY, ADJUST ACCORDINGLY AS NECESSARY

All of these themes are about your specific needs. Be clear in what they are and what your process is doing for you.

Your Daily Planner will undoubtedly help you save time while making you more effective and efficient. It will also make you more purposeful in each moment and give you rest with clear mind, knowing you have not missed any important steps.

Remember, everything counts. The little as well as the large. But the critical thing is to be aware of priorities and always strive for improvement and greater efficiency. When you see how well your daily record keeps you on track, don't forget to thank your daily planner. That's you, by the way.

> *The harder you work, the luckier you get.*
> – GARY PLAYER

17.
Luck

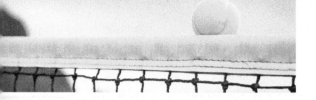

How many times have we heard, "I was so unlucky!" Or, "Luck wasn't in my corner!" Or any semblance of this overused idea—"Luck be a lady tonight," as Frank Sinatra once sang.

Good fortune and misfortune happen to all of us. This is a fact of life. But—to put a fine point on it—I am a true believer in your perspective being the navigator towards the type of "luck" you create.

Why do we let one moment of so-called bad luck change our perspective or attitude? And, in the next moment, the glass that was half-full now appears half-empty. This is merely one instance of how thinking—especially about luck and its influence—can change from positive to negative in a single heartbeat.

I say, keep the balance and perspective in your mind. Stay on an even keel, with clear thoughts of your own progress, and you will create good luck, good fortune, or whatever you want to call it.

These themes are dialed to our demeanor—good or bad, hopeful or downcast. We have discussed this in previous chapters on the type of inevitability we choose for ourselves based on the way we are looking at things.

Keep working hard, keep visualizing the execution of a good plan and make that your focal point. When you do this often enough and rigorously enough, a positive sense of inevitability will surface and you will create your opportunities, your own bountiful good luck. By being true to yourself and your vision, you can also endure misfortune in a matter of fact, no-big-deal kind of way.

I remember a brief conversation I had with Roger about the "Hawk-Eye" system, which replays pictures of where the tennis ball lands on court to determine if the ball is in or out. This machine takes human error out of the equation for the tennis players and the fans as well. Roger has not been an advocate for the system, but he has accepted its use and moved on.

There is the obvious inequity of having Hawk-Eye on *some* courts, but not all courts at tournament, thus making it an unfair measurement overall. Commenting on this, Roger said, "One call shouldn't decide a match anyway. There are many points and instances throughout a match where you could focus and bring up an argument, not just that one call. So it really doesn't win you or lose you a match."

I think this is an interesting perspective. Roger basically was saying that throughout the process, each point is equally important because it puts you in "that big moment." But in order to get there, all the other instances happen in an accumulation of previous points and create that precious moment—so each point is incredibly valuable and a ladder to success. But the full measure of win or lose is in the process—the organic, naturally-grown event at hand, not the individual point.

I think there's a valuable lesson here, and it leads us back to our process and the importance of the positive frame of mind. The theme of positivity and the mentality that comes with it will work when applied to good process, good plan, good execution and… that's when good things will happen.

The larger and more important aspect of "luck" is that it forms our disposition during a particular process. What I mean by this is that it sets the tone for how we think. So, while we are in the process of executing our plan, we are either looking forward in a positive way or we are "expecting and waiting for the wheels to fall off."

This is our choice and I think it comes dangerously close to a *victim mentality* when we think of bad luck as being just around the corner. Logically, if there is good luck, there is also bad luck. And it's the old toss of a coin fatalism that figures in here. Accepting bad luck is equally as risky as embracing good luck.

Overall, just keep to the process that follows a positive path; keep working hard and smart in that direction, and be prepared at all times for change and adaptation.

Gary Player said it all: "The harder you work the luckier you get." And I might add, the luckier you work, the harder you play.

Or, the luckier you work the more optimistically you proceed.

> **66** *Just play, play your game, like you do every day when we practice, win or lose doing what you do best.* **"**
>
> - STEVE ANNACONE

18.

My Brother the Coach

C oaching is a combination of many things and the most successful coaches find the delicate balance between a multitude of roles.

A good coach is part friend, part teacher, part disciplinarian, part parent, and part sports psychologist. The hard part is not being *one* of these—or even *all* of these—but knowing *when* it is appropriate to play *which* role at *which* time. It can get confusing sometimes.

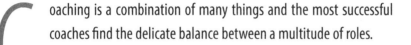

Above left: Both Michael Chang and Pete Sampras had brothers who significantly impacted their careers.

I was very fortunate to have my brother, Steve, as my traveling coach during the majority of my professional tennis career. Steve is an incredibly intelligent and aware person. Although he never competed on the professional tour, he learned the nuances of that world very quickly. In my time with him, Steve played all of the above roles and executed them with the excellence of a world class orchestra conductor. He knew just when I needed a confidence boost or just when I had to have a harsh dose of reality. He never missed a beat.

Whatever your role in life—coach of a professional athlete, teacher at a university, manager of a little league ball club—you must understand the components of your particular environment, and you need to apply the techniques that can withstand whatever pressure this environment produces.

One thing remains standard in all the different playing fields of life, and that is the importance of knowing the person you are dealing with and *understanding* how they receive the information given to them. This is vital to performance, and absolutely essential to get "buy in" from your player or pupil.

My brother Steve knew me well enough to realize that I put an incredible amount of pressure and expectation on myself. He knew that I did not respond well to foot stomping and emotional rollercoasters of explanations or directions.

One time I was playing in an event in Atlanta, Ga. As I remember, I had a bad back and this added to the usual amount of tension I experienced when in pursuit of excellence. In this case, I not only had to *play* well, I had to *be* well, and it was the latter that gave me some doubts.

Steve sensed I was focusing too much on the outcome and not enough on the moment at hand. While we were having dinner before the event, we got into a conversation about the difficulties one faces when being physically impaired. Steve said, "On top of the back problem, you've got your emotional state. And that is where you're killing yourself with expectation. You're locked into thinking about your long-term future, and how, if you don't perform well here… well, this is it!"

I nodded, taking it all in. He was right, of course. But how was I going to change the course I'd unwittingly fallen into?

Steve continued, "The great thing about tennis is there's always next week, opportunity after opportunity. You've been practicing well and your back is holding up, and you're making good progress, so just grasp the fact that, no matter what, you're going to do the best you can. All you've got to do now is stick to the strategy we're working on."

His reasoning was clear. He wasn't giving me a magic feather and telling me I could fly. He also wasn't lamenting my back injury. He was, however, telling me to stop thinking about the future.

Something clicked. I guess I was ready to hear him say something like this. At any rate, I let go of consequence and expectation and started to think only of playing. Almost immediately, I started to believe I would be fine physically, and that the result, whatever it might be, would take care of itself. I felt at peace for the first time in a while. I was excited to play, and there was no attachment to it: just playing. As it happened, I had a terrific week, getting to the finals and then losing a tough match to John McEnroe. That jump-started my process and got me going in a great direction.

This is why it's so important as a coach or mentor to know who you are dealing with and how best to help them. Steve pushed the right buttons by emphasizing my preoccupation with result. His plain-spoken advice loosened me up so I could perform without fear and without restraint. Without Steve's insistence on performance, I would've given a higher priority to my back than my backhand; I would've fallen into deeper self-doubt, further frustration, and insecurity. As it was, I banished those enemies and my back pain diminished and allowed me to play at a higher level. It was yet another lesson in the old maxim: you are what you think you are and you feel what you think you feel.

LISTENING AND CONTRIBUTING

I think it is vital for a coach to be a good listener. Unless a coach can truly hear what is going through the mind of his player, he can't grasp the best way to proceed. It's imperative that the coach understand the entire landscape—the physical, mental, and emotional map of the player's being. Here is where the best coaches shine, they sit back and listen. Then they weigh the different components and give thoughtful direction. It doesn't happen in any other order than this: listen, learn, advise.

KNOWLEDGE

Knowledge is a key ingredient for the coach. And it can come from many different areas. It can be personal, from past experience. It can be educational, as in from books, schooling, or both. And, of course, knowledge can be a fusion of all of these, with even the unexpected mystery that some insist on calling instinct. It, too, is knowledge but of an intuitive nature.

No doubt, being a coach involves a skill set. Here are some of the shorthand skills I think are part of the territory of successful coaching:

1. LEARNING THE RIGHT TECHNIQUES

2. DEALING WITH PROCESS ORIENTATION

3. CONCENTRATING ON DISCIPLINE AND FOCUS

4. SETTING UP PROCESS-ORIENTED GOALS THAT WORK

5. STRENGTHENING THE ABILITY TO DO THE ABOVE IN A SPECIFIC WORK ENVIRONMENT

6. LEARNING TO DEAL WITH ADVERSITY

7. COMPREHENDING AND BELIEVING IN THE BIG PICTURE

8. HONING THE ABILITY TO EXECUTE UNDER PRESSURE

My personal style has been an accumulation of both past experience as a tennis player and also my good fortune in learning from some really great coaches.

I grew up in a house of educators—both of my parents were schoolteachers and administrators, so perhaps it was there that I started out seeing the importance of process and focus. I like to think this was also passed down to me, that I was "listening" even as a young boy, seeing *how* things worked, and *why* through my parents' examples as much as through their personal lessons..

Later on, I was again fortunate to have such talented tennis teachers and coaches—from my first coach, Whitey Joslin, to my last, brother Steve.

As I've said earlier in this book, I grew up at the Nick Bollettieri Tennis Academy. Nick in my opinion, is the pre-eminent tennis coach on the planet. I spent nearly four years under Nick's tutelage. He was a hardcore disciplinarian who knew how to get the most out of his students. Without Nick I never would have been a professional player, nor would I have been able to understand and manage the world of coaching tennis.

In the early stages of development, the coach has to establish a primary focus in his student. And that focus, quite simply, is interest. For without interest, nothing happens. I remember sitting in one of the first meetings at Nick's camp. He was speaking with such passion. He started out by saying, "Tennis is a world of opportunity. So many things out there that can be made possible with a tennis racket." Certainly this got our attention, and then he went into low-low, his famous disciplinary four-wheel drive power gear. "Many of you are wasting your time on the practice courts and creating bad habits for yourselves. Too much fooling around, too many missed moments, too many missed practices. You have to focus, you have to be disciplined!" he said.

He went on with hardly a drawn breath. "I have had one player make it to the top professional level, Brian Gottfried. The former top two in the world and then you kids come down here and think because you are one of the best in your section of the country you have *carte blanche* and you will become a world class player, by default. NO CHANCE. I just came back from a trip to South America and saw 50 kids that have twice the desire, twice the will that you have. Let's see what you guys can do, what you can do every day… let's see how long can you do it!"

I remember leaving that meeting wondering if he was trying to kill our will or challenge us to the next level. It was so interesting to see the next practice session. The kids were sharply focused and ready to do whatever it took. Nick's speech was an injection of adrenaline. Desire was rampant and running through every one of us.

Nick's magic was potent stuff. Not only could he motivate you like no one else, but once you were up and running he wouldn't let you fall into a lull. He would be on you, driving you, but also somehow convincing you that," the world is your oyster, but you have to stay after it, you can't fade, you can't have self-doubt and self-will at the same time, you've got to will yourself to keep working. There are others that want what you want, and they'll sacrifice everything and work their asses off to get it."

While I was a student at Nick's I met one of the most important people in my life,

Coach Mike DePalmer. The head tennis coach during my time at the University of Tennessee, Coach DePalmer later developed my physical and mental skills to the point where I could become a professional tennis player.

Nick may have kindled the fire but it was Coach D who brought the flame to a white heat and pushed me from a national top 20 player under 18 years old to the No. 2 collegiate player in the country. Amazingly, he did this in just two years.

Coach D applied the drilled-in discipline from the school of Nick, but he combined it with confidence building and motivational training, both vital in professional athletics. Coach D's perspective of the athletic world is second to none, in my opinion. And his knowledge of how the mind drives the athlete is also very deep.

After my second year at the University of Tennessee, I wondered if I should turn professional or play another year. In the end, I finished the collegiate year as the No. 2 player in the country and off I went to play the professional tour as an amateur that summer.

Frankly, it was a rough summer. I lost seven weeks in a row on the professional tour in the last round of qualifying, and my confidence at the professional level was waning. Coach D, Steve, and I discussed options. We ultimately decided to take the fall semester off so I could play a couple of tournaments in Europe, then return to college in January.

I was down in the dumps after my shortcomings at the tour level. It began as a small refrain of doubt: *Am I ready? Do I really have what it takes?*

Coach D shrugged it off and said, "Seven tournaments is nothing. We are talking about a career. This is the first time you've played in that environment for any consistent period of time and you have unrealistic expectations. Forget the results. We need to keep working on your movement, your serve and your volleys. With those kicking in for you, you'll create plenty of opportunities. But remember—it's a long career and seven events is merely a blip on the radar."

It sounded simple enough. So we went back to the drawing board with Steve and pushed really hard for a few weeks before heading over to Europe. Coach D implored me to stop being such a perfectionist. I can hear him saying, "Just play, play your game, like you do every day when we practice, win or lose doing what you do best!"

When I still looked a bit doubtful, he added. "Let me break it down for you again. There are 25-30 tournaments a year—you'll have some bumps in the road... so what!"

I remember settling into my seat on the plane. *I am going off to Europe,* I told myself. That sounded a little daunting or a little daft, I'm not sure which, but it made me smile because I could hear Coach D's voice in my head. He was in there all right, as any coach should be.

By the time I arrived in Basel, Switzerland, for the qualifying tournament, I'd completely banished the memory of the seven consecutive last round defeats.

I won my first two qualifying matches.

Looking back on that now, I remember hearing the confident words and mantras of Coach D and Steve: "It's no big deal! Just play!" I felt as if a huge weight had been lifted. I slept well and the next day I went into that final round feeling good about my game. There were no unnecessary burdens attached to what *might happen,* no darkside or lightside *what-ifs to drag me down.*

I played very well, and I qualified!

Then in the main draw, I defeated a top 30 player in the world in the first round.

In the quarterfinals, however, I went up against No. 8 in the world, Vitas Gerulaitis. I lost in the tie-breaker in the third and deciding set.

But the important thing was that I heard Coach D: "No big deal. There's nothing but opportunities ahead."

And so I left Basel saying to myself, and knowing it was true. *I can do this! But I have to maintain that mental balance. I have to mold my mind to just play so that I have positive reactions to failure and success.*

During my train ride to Paris, I had a feeling of lightness and joy but Coach D's words kept re-playing in my mind: "There are 25-30 tournaments a year—you will have some bumps in the road… so what!"

I knew the double-edged sword of mental indecision. It was sharp both ways and could cut confidence in two.

So I worked on one thing: "Keep the balance." I repeated this to myself over and over, and it helped.

My brother Steve and Coach D worked together to push me up the ranks. I owe a great deal to both of them, but Steve especially because he dedicated much of his life to traveling more than 30 weeks a year on tour to make sure it was "done right" and to keep me focused on the court and give me balance and objectivity when we were on the road.

Steve is one of the most generous, selfless people I know and without him managing the day-to-day development of my evolution, I would've floundered in mediocrity. But I shouldn't forget the other coaches who have contributed to my journey: Andre Dupre, Paul Masters, and Don Brosseau, to name a few. It's difficult to put a finger precisely on where each of my mentors made his contribution but the combination of their skill-sets galvanized one single message I shall never forget: Go for the full extent, reach your full potential!

EVOLUTION

I am a firm believer in the idea that as humans we accumulate a lot of baggage. Good and bad. We go on our journey and we carry a lot of bags, some of them given to us without our knowledge, but we heft them anyway, as if it were our due.

This is why it's so important to build good habits as you are learning. Once you're older it's difficult to rid yourself of the baggage that you didn't even know you were carrying.

How can you react quickly and spontaneously when you are carrying a lot of stuff that weighs you down? You have to be free in the moment to make the right decisions.

I have watched Pete Sampras in the most pressure-packed situations a tennis player could ever face.

What did he do?

He was so structurally sound, that in most situations, there was no baggage.

But this is not to say he didn't have any. And I do not mean to imply that Pete was successful in every pressure packed scenario. But when the pressure was on, Pete could count on his *default mode* allowing him to execute his own strategy. Ultimately, he might win or lose… but on his terms.

Some less talented, less established players that I worked with had what I would call clouded or unclear default modes.

With these types of players, when the pressure is presented or adversity strikes, their old habits kick in and the baggage shows up.

"Man, was I unlucky!"

"I got a terrible line call."

"I always get hurt in the big moments."

Such thoughts are defense mechanisms. Part of the baggage/bad habit process that seems to help with pressure is actually the cause of some of it. At the end of the day, it doesn't matter what the thought is. If, it gets you away from emphasizing your focus on the process, it is destructive.

As a coach, I think that early development in dealing with stress is crucial. You must help young people cope with adversity so this skill will flourish as they get older and become more efficient at their trade.

CHALLENGES OF FAMILY COACHING

While it is usually helpful to have family and close friends there to help guide us, it can also be complicated.

One of the key components of being a successful coach is to the ability to be objective. We have also talked about how this can help the coach sift through certain emotional environments, and thus navigate in a positive way.

I know as a father I have had my own challenges. And it's not always easy to step back, survey the situation, and then offer concise direction without at least some emotional response as well. It's only natural that emotions have a way of creeping into most conversations.

In tennis we've seen some unusually successful parent and sibling situations. We've seen, and perhaps admired, Richard Williams, father of Venus and Serena. Or Martina Hingis' mother, Melanie, or Jennifer Capriati's father, Stefano, when she was at the top of her game.

In these instances, I would say the parents did many things very well and helped to create some outstanding habits. I would also say that these are unique individuals with extraordinary talents. The balance here is delicate, the margins are narrow. Again, the double-edged sword.

When coaching a family member, I would caution you to be careful and thoughtful at all times, because you may think you're helping to remove baggage but in reality, you are just loading it up in a different way. If you have a family member coach or are considering becoming one, it may be best to use the following guidelines:

TRY THESE HELPFUL HINTS:

1. REMAIN OBJECTIVE

2. BE PASSIONATE, BUT NOT IRRATIONAL

3. BE CLEAR ABOUT THE DIRECTION AND HABITS

4. UNDERSTAND THE BIG PICTURE

5. MAKE SURE THE ARENA YOU ARE IN IS THE
CHOICE OF THE PUPIL
RATHER THAN YOUR OWN CHOICE

6. GIVE BALANCE (MAINTAIN YOUR OWN)

7. SEEK SOUND ADVICE FROM OTHERS

To sum up, the coach's overall job is a tough one. Whether it is your son or daughter, a friend, student, or just someone you work with who is learning the ropes from his mentor, you will have your hands full just being that multi-tasking, multi-talented person, the hard-to-be-with, the hard-to-be-without guy or gal we call Coach.

" *What noise?* **"**
– TIM GULLIKSON

19.

Manage Your Environment

Your environment changes and evolves as often as you do. And even if the physical environment remains stable, there will be task changes, expectation changes, perception changes, and goal changes. Nothing remains constant except change itself.

Yet each new environment, while sometimes puzzling at first, creates different challenges for us. For instance, when I was starting my life as a professional tennis player I embarked on a very interesting first "leap" onto the world's stage.

I'd just finished my third year of collegiate tennis and I entered the qualifying tournament at Wimbledon with much excitement and very little expectation. Mostly, I was a sponge soaking up my new environment.

But before I knew it, I had won three matches and had qualified for the main event. After winning four more matches, I was all of a sudden preparing to play a man I'd idolized as a kid. I was on the draw sheet opposite Jimmy Connors in the quarterfinals of the event.

This was my first match on the hallowed grounds of the Centre Court at Wimbledon, and I didn't quite know what to expect. I had my friends and support group there, including my brother/coach advising me on how to handle the scenario, and it seemed like a lot to digest. But I honestly felt OK, and was thoroughly enthused about the opportunity that lay before me.

The day of the match came and it was a little hectic, especially with the media's interest in me as a new player to reach the last eight in the tournament. It was my first time seeing it at this level but my warm up was good and all my preparations seemed on target.

Prior to a match on Centre Court, you wait in a tiny white room just underneath the court's entrance, and then both players walk on to the court.

I met Jimmy Connors for the first time in that tiny white room, and it was cordial and fine. As we walked on the court we turned, stopped, and bowed to the royal box. We started our warm up and all seemed right to me. There was lots of noise and a frenetic buzz in the air, but I felt comfortable and ready for the challenge.

After we warmed up our serves, and the umpire announced, "Players ready? Play!" And at that precise moment, there was an absolute deafening silence. To this day, that infinite quiet, so quickly achieved, resonates in my mind. That was the first time in my life I'd experienced anything like it—It went from buzzing, chatting people getting situated to a dead silence on the tennis world's largest and, some would say, most challenging stage.

I remember thinking: *How am I going to deal with this new environment?*

My moment of paralysis lasted a few fleeting moments, but to this day I remember that initial feeling. It was so difficult to focus on the task at hand and the process I was about to undertake. My environment had enveloped me. No thought, no plan, no process—just paralysis.

After that moment passed, I was back to "just playing," but the effect was palpable and could have been traumatic if I had not been told that this could, and did, happen to others. Maybe in that split-second recognition, I realized no one is invulnerable to the environment he is in—no matter how well-coached or prepared, environment is an ingredient and we must be aware and thoughtful in order to deal with it.

Unfortunately, even though I snapped into shape and played my best tennis—or the best tennis of which I was capable at that time—I lost to the better man on that particular day. But nonetheless, it was a great experience and one I will never forget.

This may be an extreme example of how our environment can swallow us up. It may not overcome us completely, but it can definitely have a huge impact on what we are trying to accomplish. Awareness is a key component of managing your environment. Because I was expecting something of a unique experience, my paralysis was only momentary and my old habits of regaining composure and clarity kicked in.

How do the "best of the best" maintain and sustain through environmental changes? Is it inherent confidence? Does that even exist? Is it something learned or perhaps something born?

If it is learned behavior, how do we summon it in a time of need?

Well, I believe the best players all seem to have it. First of all, they believe in themselves implicitly and they find a way, no matter what the environment is, to overcome the odds. I've seen Pete Sampras find a way to win on the main stage at the U.S. Open after vomiting on the court from exhaustion. How? How does one take and give back that which the environment pitches at us?

It is partially inherent, I think. And it is also partially learned. But mostly it's done with hard work, dedication, steely focus, and iron-clad belief.

We all have these components inside us, we just have to access them and make the good habits come to the fore while overriding the unpredictable elements of our environment. This is often typified in cliché "coach-talk" as, "When the going gets tough, the tough get going."

The default mode, in athletics and in life is a sudden reversion to habits, which brings up the following questions you can ask yourself:

1. ARE MY WORK HABITS GOOD?

2. IS MY FOCUS ON THE TASK AT HAND STRONG AND CLEAR?

3. AM I ABLE TO ZERO IN ON MY PROCESS DAY-IN AND DAY-OUT AT PRACTICE OR AT WORK?

4. CAN I DEAL WITH ADVERSITY WELL ENOUGH TO SIFT THROUGH THE DRAMA, WHATEVER IT MIGHT BE, AND GET BACK TO MY PROCESS?

If you can answer these in the affirmative, you are on track. If not, where do you come up short? Address the issues and refocus to get yourself in a state of mind that will allow you to build a good base, so when a pressure-filled environment is present, you naturally revert to good habits rather than bad ones. The most important part here is to be able to sift through the emotional warp that is usually present in a rough environment.

SELF-SABOTAGE

Self-sabotage is a characteristic that many of us have and it can surface in numerous ways. The bottom line is, no matter what the problem is, you may unconsciously derail yourself from the process and the path of success, if you allow self-sabotage in.

Most self-sabotage comes from the mind. It is the glass half-full, the "uh-oh, here we go again" theme. No matter how you describe the thought as it comes on, it's definitely not the process-oriented and planned thought that is needed to win the day. Contrarily, it's the thing that closes down the day for you.

I used to have this problem. During my college career, I started working with a sports psychologist, Dr. Noel Blundell. Noel is an Australian practitioner and remains one of my dearest friends.

In his own special way, Noel got into my head and explained to me how quickly I would mount expectation (pressure) on myself and how my positive energy would be focused on a perception of a result instead of a well-planned process. This was a form of self-sabotage, he said, and also a characteristic I needed to manage in order to deal with my environment.

Noel worked with me and really helped me to come up with some specific exercises to refocus on my process and to flush out all erroneous thoughts. The one key exercise Noel taught me was a breathing exercise where I focused on my abdominal muscles. I was advised to think of and visualize them expanding and contacting as I breathed. This was a catalyst that dropped my heart rate and got my mind clear and enabled me to relax and stay on the next point and its own unfolding plan.

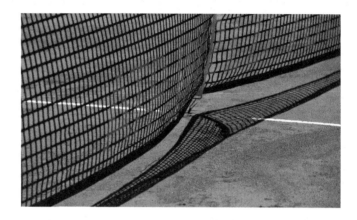

The mind leads the body. Let the mind flush out the self-sabotage illusions and hold on to the positive theme of reality. This automatically brings forward the process at hand.

There are times, of course, when we get into a downward spiral from this self-sabotage thing and it seems like the harder we try, the further away we get from our goal. *How do I accentuate the positive when everything seems to be going negative?*

These are the moments where we have a choice. We can either be an advocate for emotional change and push the process in the right direction, or we can embrace the illusion and succumb to the adversity. This is a rational, not an emotional, choice and it takes discipline and self-belief to deal with this when you are in crisis mode. Most importantly, finding this moment of balance takes practice! Our process-engine, if you will, needs an injection of high-octane optimism.

Noel used to tell me that we should deal with our emotions first, and clear the mind so that the hard work we produce in practice can come out in the match. Same with life, same with work. We have to set up the "right practice" so that when the pressure is on, the emotional reaction recedes, and the optimistic plan proceeds. Noel's breathing exercise was the catalyst that calmed me, cleared my mind, and got me back to my game plan.

Sounds so easy, doesn't it?

Yet when we're in the crunch of temperament, and frustration is near, when anger and disappointment are driving us, it isn't easy to breathe deeply and turn the page back to the winning scenario. Hard though as it was for me to do this, I learned through practice to remain objective in the face of adversity. And that has made all difference to me as a player and as a coach.

EMOTIONAL PROS AND CONS

Emotion shouldn't be considered negative. It's the key component that drives us. Some need more than others, some use it as a positive, some as a negative, but all of us use it.

Each of us has to find the right level on our personal barometer. Emotion is fine, just don't let it rule you, don't let it drive your process and cloud your *decision* into *indecision*. There are very few people who can let emotion be a constant in their process and still get the most out of themselves.

Usually, untrained, or raw, emotion becomes, at the very least, an ingredient of self-sabotage. Be aware of your levels. Take stock in how you have operated in the past and when, where, and how you have become most successful. These themes are important because the feeling of the emotion can be a terrific asset or a great hindrance.

John McEnroe was a very volatile athlete and he was able to use this as a catalyst many times. I saw this first-hand. John and I were playing in Chicago during my first year on tour and I had won the first set and was ahead 4-2 in the second set when he went on a tirade at the umpire. This was a significant delay and he was very emotional and he was very sure he was correct.

Yet even after losing his temper, John remained overheated and emotionally charged during the next few moments of the match—this is just the thing I've been warning against! He gradually got better and better and beat me pretty handily in the third set. I was so amazed he was able to harness this frustration and anger and not let it affect what he was trying to do on court. John is that rare exception to the rule—a man who was, at certain times, able to alchemize his frustration and anger and turn it to passion and successful execution. While it is exciting to see someone like this, it brings to mind the phrase: "Please don't try this at home."

However, long story short: know your barometer for emotional passion, and act accordingly. Your environment, nine times out of 10, is you. Which is why Tim Gullikson missed the distracting airplanes flying overhead and said later, "What noise?"

66 *For the future the best preparation is an unafraid today.* **99**
— DR. FRANK CRANE

20.

The Ultimate Challenge

've gone through this book preaching about process, focus, planning, balance, objectivity, but now I'm wondering: is there such a thing as the ultimate challenge? That is beyond the obvious, the goal. We all go through so many things in life, professionally and personally, and that's why I have spoken so often about sticking to the process, which is both the anchor that will steady you and the air balloon that will lift you off.

I want to walk around this subject of the ultimate challenge a little bit. I would say that, for most of us, our general response to situations is countered by habit. Habits make up who we are and how we deal with things. And, further, habits show us conclusively why process is so important. For without it, bad habits don't die. And good habits aren't born. The higher the drama, or the more consequential the perceived result, the more difficult it is to deal with any sudden or ongoing situation.

Knowing this to be true, I would say that *any* and *every* challenge is the ultimate challenge. Your first interview for a big job, your first competitive game, your first day at a new job—all of these seem equally important at the time.

As we get older I think the natural reaction is that time is crucial and opportunities are more rare. Once again, this can create expectation and pressure, and it's the reason why those who have a good process in place find it possible to deal with new challenges more easily.

Towards the end of my playing career, I felt much more pressure because I could see the window closing, so to speak.

I remember talking with Roger in December 2011 about his difficult loss in the semifinal of the previous U.S. Open where he held two match points against Novak Djokovic and was unable to convert.

"You've had a great run this fall after the U.S. Open," I told him. "But I wonder what the key factor was in your rebound from that match?"

"I don't like to lose," Roger explained. "It's no fun, especially in those scenarios, but winning or losing is not going to change who I am or how I feel about myself and my life. I have won plenty and I know sports can be really tough sometimes, but I love being there and there's more to come. So, I just have to be ready and keep working, and next time, I will be on the other end."

Sounds easy, right?

Ah, but perhaps the ultimate challenge is this: How can I react that way no matter what's happened, and no matter what the perceived consequence is? How do I educate myself to have that constancy, that well-balanced perspective? How do I keep from being frustrated and disappointed? How do I maintain objectivity and educate myself to the reality of what happened/what's happening?

Well, the answer is in all of the process-related advice in this book; in all of the ways to stay on target. The wall of adversity is always your ultimate challenge. But so is the mundane wall of every day.

In a recent conversation with Coach DePalmer I asked him what his ultimate challenge is.

Coach D said, "In life, it's all phases, that's the challenge, understanding that at different times, it's different things that seem so important. 54 years ago, it was: How am I going to make this marriage and family life what my wife and I need it to be? Then, later on, how am I going to raise our kids the best possible way to have a happy, healthy life? Then: How am I going to make my club and my work with Nick at the academy what we want it to be? Then: How am I going to help the University of Tennessee win a NCAA tennis championship?

"My point is, all of those were *ultimate!* All of them demanded great focus, great perspective. But Paul, the most important thing is how you manage each one. Because they are all connected—sports, life, tennis etc. Your ultimate challenge (or any challenge) is your reaction to your environment, who's around you, who's having an impact on you, who you are listening to… all of these have a similarity, whether in sports or life. If you have good character, good work ethic, and a history of good perspective, and thoughtful reactions to problem solving, you probably will be successful at tackling your challenges."

Typical Coach D. Thoughtful, passionate, and spot on. He just knows that it is habit and history that guide us and that determine our reaction to things. We need to be ahead of the curve to make sure we are prepared to tackle whatever challenge comes up.

It's easy to forget how valuable experience can be. When I have the opportunity to speak with objective people who have been through many different situations in life, they often rely on "thoughtful understanding" to explain their points of view. You often hear wise elders say, "Experience is the best teacher." And some say, "It's the *only* teacher." The wisest say, "It's easy to learn from your own mistakes; the trick is to learn from someone else's."

Coach DePalmer was perfectly clear when he said, *"Everything is important."*

Players like Pete and Roger take winning and losing in stride. The outcome of a match did not, and does not, dent their confidence or pump it up. Nor does it have an effect on their daily process. Their sense of self, their understanding of who they are and what they can do, is their equilibrium as competitive athletes. What for some might be the daily grind, for them, it's "the daily mind." I see so many athletes today who dwell on words like *never* and *always,* thus sealing themselves into habitual speculation about what they're doing.

This is a pet peeve of my wife, Elisabeth—the *never and always attitude.* When we get emotional and off-message we go global and we characterize in an exaggerated manner. Many a self-fulfilling negative prophecy was laid down as law on the courts of Never and Always.

However, in my post-tournament conversations with Pete and Roger, we often talked about loss and what it meant, but they viewed this with objectivity. The loss did not hurt less because they understood it but their resilience was equal to the high volatility of the game.

It is all a game, if you can learn to see it that way. And it is all the ultimate challenge, if you can play it that way.

Coach DePalmer's lessons of life and tennis have been a guiding light through trying times and his words of wisdom continue to resonate. Thanks, Coach.

Epilogue

 *It ain't over 'til it's over."*
- YOGI BERRA

W hen I read books, I try to categorize and characterize their content and theme. That way, I get the most out of them, and I remember them long after I have finished reading too. When I started writing, I knew that what I was aiming for was a kind of recipe book. One that would be about fulfillment, and as a result, success.

Right away I saw that each chapter was another ingredient. Add all of the correct ingredients together, and I'd have the complete recipe. Not an easy task, especially in a world where the sports environment, just like the world, is constantly changing. My ingredients and overall recipe needed to be adaptive.

So I decided to draw on my personal experiences with some of the best tennis players in the history of the game. This would be a terrific way to watch the evolution of the game, and more importantly, to observe the personality traits that made the game what it is today.

Coaching For Life shows us the key areas of focus that help us to pursue our own dreams—whatever they may be. The goal here is to know how best to apply our actions so that you move smoothly in the right direction.

Some books I have seen get caught up in results. *How to make a million while drinking coffee. How to get rich while you sleep.* Result-oriented formulas are often hasty and over-generalized. This happens when the pot of gold at the end of the rainbow is the only thing that is emphasized.

In *Coaching For Life,* the all-or-nothing-win principle is what causes loss of focus, not gain of gold.

Instead, I have emphasized such concepts as Process, Power of Belief and Positive Sense of Inevitability to drive our journey. While going forward, the Daily Planner is an up to date witness of our progress and a counterbalance to loss of focus. By utilizing all of these things we can stay in the now and know that today's applications will lead to tomorrow's results.

I have also shown the different ways of dealing with adversity and how to adjust and adapt when situations turn. This helps to maximize your individual potential.

Throughout the book, I have underscored that it doesn't matter if you are playing tennis, throwing darts, or mowing the lawn…it doesn't matter if you are teaching an English class or studying plants as a botanist. In all walks of life you should feel good about what you are doing. And you should always strive to maximize your potential.

It sounds so easy when you state it in a book. But in practical terms, in living your life, it's not easy. We must face the daily challenges—those everyday barriers that block our ability to attain our goals—with equanimity and poise. And, once achieving this, I have often mentioned how important it is to use a process that gives enjoyment and allows you to appreciate the journey.

I have also spent time discussing the big picture and how, when you ignore it and remain fixed on the lesser goal—the small picture, wins or losses, fortune or luck—all of these tend to make you feel less confident in yourself, and this can ultimately send you into a negative, downward spiral.

Making sure you have reasonable expectations is a huge component in allowing your personal process to reach the desired result. Reasonable expectations and a realistic time frame allow you to go through your process with a good perspective and a positive sense of inevitability.

In writing of the power of process, system, planning and focus, it is important to remember the variable of the emotional roller coaster that exists in all of us. This is something that can either be used as a positive driving force, or if we are not in control of it, a sudden and precipitous downfall. The emotional part of the journey is an integral part of the process; it can often be harnessed and used properly. But when it forces you into illogical decisions that are not backed up by fact and evidence, emotion can be an enemy. Best that you use that emotion to drive you in your discipline and be the catalyst in your daily routine.

Coaching for Life is not a rigid book of rules applicable to every situation—a one size fits all. Rather, it is a book of process that enables you to change your course of action as you see fit, to adapt and improvise according to a consistent plan that fits your specific needs as an individual. This is a book of life that emphasizes living it, embracing it, and making sure we do everything we can to get out of it what we want, what we need, and what will be best for the kind of person we wish to be. And remember: it ain't over even when it's over.

Acknowledgments

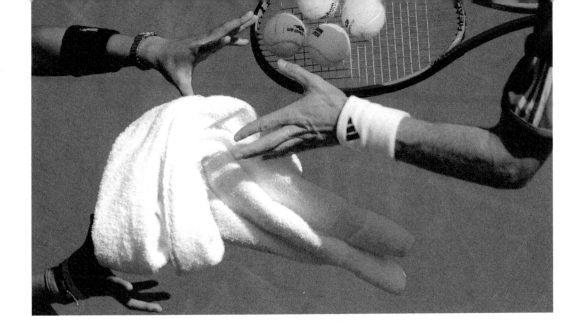

have been fortunate to have many people help or advise on this book, which has gone through various stages over a period of years as time allowed.

Thanks to Dr. Roetert for his time and help with this project, as always a pleasure to collaborate with you, Paul.

Mariah, thank you for your patience and vision in laying out the format and being the architect of the content.

Gerald, without your skills and patience this book wouldn't have happened. Thanks for your guidance and hard work, it has been a terrific process thanks to you.

My coaching career has had a vast array of participants and, again, I have been very fortunate. There have been quite a number of players from whom I've learned and spent time, but I truly need to thank those players who, for a long period of time, let me see from the front row what they were—and are—capable of. Pete, Tim, Sloane and Roger—you've allowed me to participate in your process and you've taught me a great deal. I thank you for the room with a view!

We all go through trials and tribulations, and some are more relevant than others, and sometimes I am embarrassed by what I think are important issues in my life and how I can dwell on them. Through the trials and tribulations, I have had a family with overflowing support and love.

Through clarity and clouds, my wife, Elisabeth, has been there as an inspiration, coach, friend, partner, and guiding light. You have given me the courage to write and to embrace life's journey with a smile. Thank you, E.

As I go through each chapter of the book, I think about my children. They embody the youthful exuberance, the pursuit of dreams common to all of us. Nick, Liv, and Emmett, you bring me joy every day and I look forward to watching your constant growth and change with pride and joy.

My parents: you have been there watching, both from afar and up close and personal. You've seen the good, the bad, and the ugly, and have always been supportive and loving. You've taught me so much, while also giving me the room to grow into who I am today and who I'll be tomorrow. Thanks, Mom and Dad.

Shirley and Cary, you know how much your support and love over the years means to me. You and the kids have been there for so long and through so much. My love goes out to you, and thank you.

My brother Steve has never gotten enough credit for all he did as my coach. He was the one that steadied the ship, the one that brought perspective and thoughtful wisdom to my life as a young player. That in and of itself is quite an accomplishment, but doing this while being my brother, friend, and confidant, and dealing with all of the turbulence that surrounds the journey, makes it quite a challenge. Thanks, Steve.

Coach DePalmer, you've played the many roles I discuss in the book: coach, father, friend, and advisor, and all this while teaching me, making me believe, and helping me realize that life and opportunity are what we make of them not what we take from them. While I am out on the road coaching today, your words—Coach D's words of wisdom— resonate in my head all the time. Thanks, Coach.

I'm not sure where to start with you, Nick. You took me in at age 14 and watched me mature from a flaky adolescent to a professional tennis player, to a coach. You always made time for me and gave of yourself generously. Nick, you are a gem and I thank you from the bottom of my heart.

As an inconsistent college student who was trying hard to understand what he was getting into as a tennis player, I needed the guidance of someone who understood the psychology of the professional athlete. Dr. Noel Blundell, you were the one who helped me when I needed you. And Noel, you've been a dear friend and an incredible advisor for over 25 years and I can't thank you and your family enough for all you've done.

For all the wonderful photos, a special thanks to Ray Giubilo (Tennisphotographer. com); Marianne Bevis (flickr.com/photos/mariannebevis); Michael Baz Photography; Peter McCabe (PeterMcCabephotography.com), Danny Moloshok (molophoto.com) and Stephanie Myles.

For all those that have helped me down the road I don't even know how to say thank you. Whitey Joslin, Andre Dupre, Paul Masters, Don Brosseau, and Bill Shelton, just to name a few. You have all shaped me and given me the ingredients that have formulated *Coaching For Life*.

And what about all my friends, fellow players, peers—most importantly, my long time doubles partner Christo Van Rensburg, a dear friend who put up with all my nonsense for many years. We had such great times and I thank you for your expertise but more than that, for the friendship. And to each and all, thanks again for bringing me to the realization that there isn't "a way," there are many ways, but within each way is the process that gets you there. Be true to that process, and as my father once said, "exhaust all your resources" in the pursuit of excellence and happiness. In the end, I must be honest and thank the process itself.

CPSIA information can be obtained
at www.ICGtesting.com
Printed in the USA
BVOW05*0916161217
6102BVAU00018B/19/P